SOUTHEAST ASIAN FAMILIES AND POOLED LABOR

MULTIPLE WAGE-EARNER STRATEGIES FOR REFUGEE HOUSEHOLDS IN THE U.S.

KIYOUNG LEE

GARLAND PUBLISHING, INC.
A MEMBER OF THE TAYLOR & FRANCIS GROUP
NEW YORK & LONDON / 1998

Library of Congress Cataloging-in-Publication Data

Lee, Kiyoung, 1964–
    Southeast Asian families and pooled labor : multiple wage-earner strategies for refugee households in the U.S. / Kiyoung Lee.
        p.   cm. — (Garland studies in this history of American labor)
    Includes bibliographical references and index.
    ISBN 0-8153-3216-5 (alk. paper)
    1. Southeast Asians—Employment—United States.
2. Refugees—Employment—United States. 3. Family—Economic aspects—United States. I. Title. II. Series.
HD8081.A8L43 1998
331.6'259073—dc21
                                                            98-37492

Printed on acid-free, 250-year-life paper
Manufactured in the United States of America

To my mother, Mal-Lan Kim

Contents

Tables

Preface

Refugee resettlement is rarely a new issue in the United States, which have relatively a long history of refugee-acceptance. Nowadays, however, the issue is being frequently treated as one of the important research agenda in various areas such as social work, sociology, and anthropology for inquiring their new-life experiences in American society. Policy planners in the federal, state, and local level are still concerned about the future of those refugees.

Southeast Asian refugees are not exceptional in that they have difficulty in the process of resettlement. Governments at various level and voluntary agencies attempt to assist them in achieving their self-sufficiency and in promoting their social, and cultural adjustment to American society. However, the fruits of the struggles have not been very impressive. Some attribute Southeast Asian refugees' poor adjustment to recent arrivals' lower socio-economic backgrounds than their predecessors. Also, some criticize current policy and practices of refugee resettlement assistance for their unsuccessful resettlement. Despite many successful stories of prior Vietnamese refugees in American society, today's Southeast Asian refugees are considered as a target population of public assistance and as a concerned people by American taxpayers.

The generation of multiple earners in refugee households has recently been emphasized as a policy for enhancing economic status of refugee households and encouraging exits from the receipt of public assistance. This policy is particularly important for Southeast Asian (SEA) refugee households, which are known to be poor in their labor force status and to rely extensively on public assistance compared to other ethnic or nativity cohorts among refugee populations in the

United States. However, I believe, there has rarely been research which can provide theoretical and empirical basis for the policy directive of generation of multiple earners in refugee households.

This book analyzes an inner structure of wage-labor pooling and strategies of generating wage-earner(s) among Southeast Asian refugee households rather than examines current refugee assistance programs. What is the prevailing composition of multiple earners and what factors can significantly contribute to the generation of multiple wage-earners in SEA refugee households? The analysis method is based on the belief that an individual's economic well-being generally depends on the whole household economy.

The purpose of this study appears to coincide with current refugee assistance policy, which emphasizes generating as many wage-earners as possible in a refugee household. I do not deny this view. I intend to provide policy and program designers with more clear facts related to wage-labor pooling among Southeast Asian refugee households. However, this is not the statement that I am fond of current policy directives. I cannot escape from the dispute between pros and cons arguing the time-period of federal or state assistance for refugees (i.e., how long should refugee assistance service be provided?) if generation of multiple wage-earners is viewed as one of the refugee household strategies encouraged by policy makers who emphasize an emergent and short-term assistance stressing early employment. For this matter, however, we do not have a conclusion. I think that this issue must be further studied.

This book has several implications in the research and practice on refugee resettlement in the United States. Despite the fact that this book is based on cross-sectional data analysis, analysis design of the book assumes a dynamic approach in that it analyzes not individuals but the household and consequently includes every household member in the analyses. This kind of study is expected to be better than a study based on individuals in the illustration of the household strategy of generating wage-earners. This is because that economic outcomes of individual refugees are conditioned by the characteristics of the household to which she or he belongs. The importance of a family or household has often been stressed in studying Southeast Asian refugees' economic adjustment process. Haines (1988) emphasizes that "the linkage of household structure to economic situations . . . places refugee resettlement within the wider framework of household economic strategies" (p. 12). Kibria (1994), in an ethnographic study of Vietnamese refugees in Philadelphia, also stresses that "analyses that focus on variations in household and family organization . . . may be particularly useful in generating explanations for different patterns of economic adaptation"(p. 82). Potocky's suggestion (1996) for research on "refugees' micro-level social systems" such as households is also congruent with the conceptual framework of this study.

Examination of multiple wage-earners strategies represents a meaningful alternative to study of refugees' longer-term economic outcomes such as public assistance utilization, household income, or poverty status. One prior study of SEA refugees indicates that as the number of jobs per household increases a household is more likely to be above the poverty level (Caplan, Whitmore, and Bui, 1985). Their research findings provide empirical evidence that the multiple earner strategy can make up for the labor market disadvantage of individual refugees.

This book also examines the role of human capital in accounting for the generation of multiple wage-earners in the Southeast Asian refugee household. By using aggregated and averaged values of each kind of human capital such as education, English proficiency, and job training for all adult household members, this book examines the significance of pooled household human resources for economic outcomes. It also provides evidence about the comparative value of human capital and household structure for generating multiple wage-earners in the SEA refugee household.

The contents of the book contributes valuable information with implications for resettlement to Southeast Asian refugees in the initial years following their arrival in the U.S. As shown above, this research includes only refugees who have lived in this country for less than 5 years. The importance of the initial period in Southeast Asian refugees' economic adjustment has frequently been cited in documents. The Office of Refugee Resettlement's experience of working with refugees in the U.S. "indicates that the greatest impact that services can have on a refugees' social adjustment and economic well-being occurs during a refugees' initial years" and that consequently "the refugee program must concentrate its resources on recent arrivals" (ORR, 1995, p. 72). Potocky and McDonald (1995) commented that much of the later economic status of Southeast Asian refugees is determined by their status early after arrival. More specifically, evidence suggests, "if a refugee is not working within 12 months in [the U.S.], the chance of that refugee being at work after 5 years here is only five percent"(U.S. Committee for Refugees, 1992, p. 6). Therefore, a study of labor force status and the multiple-earner generating mechanism of SEA refugee households in the initial years (approximately less than 5 years) has important implications for their long-term economic adjustment.

Finally, this study of Southeast Asian refugees can also contribute to the study of ethnic minorities. As Pedraza (1994) pointed out, it is the time "to collapse the wall" between the study of immigrants and the study of racial minorities. Considering the increasing interest in immigrants and ethnic groups in the United States, Southeast Asian refugees should not be excluded. It would be valuable for the future to analyze and generalize their initial labor market experience.

This book is divided into six chapters. Chapter 1 opens this book with an introduction of refugee resettlement, particularly for Southeast Asian refugees in the United States. This chapter includes presentation of Southeast Asian refugees' problems in the labor market, objectives of the study, and specific research questions to be examined in the book. Also, a brief introduction of current refugee assistance programs in the United States is presented in the last section of this chapter.

Chapter 2 reviews theoretical and empirical backgrounds for family wage-labor pooling, household structural approach of economic adjustment, and other related factors to Southeast Asian refugees' resettlement in the United States. Also, several important terms used in this book are defined in this chapter.

Chapter 3 is for describing research methodology of the study. This includes sampling and data collection procedure conducted by the Office of Refugee Resettlement. Comprehensive description of the contents of the data, research design, and measurement (including independent and dependent variables) follows. Also, remaining space of this chapter is spent to explain two important criteria of determining the quality of research design, i.e., validity and reliability, data transformation procedure, and data analysis methods.

Chapter 4 provides us with the results of data analysis, which presents characteristics of Southeast Asian refugee households, family status and labor status of household members, composition of wage-earners among the households, and important factors associated with the generation of multiple wage-earners.

Chapter 5 summarizes the research findings, and discusses for several significant points including role of adult children among Southeast refugee households, factors related to wage-earner generation, and the meaning of the existence of multiple earners in the Southeast Asian refugee households.

Chapter 6 presents policy and practice implications for refugee resettlement.

Acknowledgments

I believe that the completion of this study was made possible by the grace of God.

I wish to thank all the people who helped and encouraged me to finish this study. First, I wish to sincerely thank my advisor Dr. Celeste Burke, and other two committee members for my Ph. D. dissertation, Dr. Beverly Toomey, and Dr. Virginia Richardson at the Ohio State University, for their intellectual and emotional support, encouragement, and guidance in conducting this research. I am grateful to Joseph J. Gagnier, a statistician at the Office of Refugee Resettlement in Washington, D.C., for providing the data used for this research and answering my numerous questions on the data. I am indebted to Dr. Sharyn Talbert for her sincere administrative support related to all official processes for doctoral study at the Ohio State University.

Finally, I wish to thank all of my family: my parents, my brother and sisters, my wife Eunjin, and my daughter Clara, who always love me. My special thanks to my mother-in-law Jung-Hyun Kwon, who prays everyday for my family and has supported us.

Southeast Asian Familes
and Pooled Labor

CHAPTER 1

Introduction of SEA Refugees' Economic Adjustment

Refugees comprise a significant proportion of the immigrant population in the United States. Since admitting a large number of Vietnamese refugees in 1975, the United States has become one of the largest host nations for Southeast Asian (SEA) refugees. During last two decades, about 1.5 million Southeast Asian refugees entered and resettled in the United States. Although nowadays the ethnicity or nativity of refugees arriving in the United States is more varied, Southeast Asian refugees are still the largest ethnic group among the refugees in the United States

    Recently arrived Southeast Asian refugees are known to be poor in terms of their socioeconomic backgrounds and have little education, poor language ability, and few occupational skills. Given the characteristics of recent refugees, the public is much concerned about the economic outcomes for Southeast Asian refugees and their potential use of increasingly limited welfare benefits in the United States.[1] It is demonstrated that refugees will get a job as soon as possible after arrival and achieve economic self- sufficiency. However, recently arrived Southeast Asian refugees, in general, have poor economic adjustment during at least the early resettlement period. According to statistics (ORR, 1995), compared to other ethnic or nationality groups, Southeast Asian refugees have shown relatively low labor force participation, high unemployment rates, and extensive use of public assistance during the first five years after arrival.

    Current refugee resettlement policy reflects concern about the poor economic adjustment of Southeast Asian refugees. More emphasis is placed on achieving self-sufficiency through "work" than at any previous time . Also, the target of resettlement services has changed a focus on individuals to the whole family. The director's message in a Report to Congress specifies the direction of current policy for refugee resettlement: "It is paramount that service providers focus on the family rather than the individual and that employability plans seek to move the entire family to economic self-sufficiency" (ORR, 1995). To achieve this policy goal, "multiple wage-earner strategies in which more than one wage-earner in a family is helped to find a job" is stressed as an effective method.

Despite this policy emphasis, few studies have examined the issues related to multiple earner strategies or wage labor compositions of Southeast Asian refugee households. Prior research has primarily concentrated on the labor force or economic status of individual refugees rather than a whole household. In this approach, the labor force participation or employment status of individual household members as a component of household economy or household wage-labor pooling was underestimated. In other words, studies analyzing individuals make it difficult to get a comprehensive picture of the labor force status of all household members, that represents the experience of Southeast Asian refugee households in the United States.

The generation of multiple earners is a concept of a household rather than an individual. In order to better understand who are the earners or potential earners in a household and to identify factors that are associated with multiple earners, a household must be used as the unit or level of analysis. In the household composition of labor force, individual household members can be meaningful as actual or potential sources of labor.

This book concentrates on analyzing the data about labor force participation of Southeast Asian refugee households in an effort to search for significant factors for such households related to the presence of multiple wage-earners. In this context, the findings of this study may provide a better understanding of wage-labor pooling among Southeast Asian refugee households.

PROBLEM STATEMENT

According to the Annual Reports from the Office of Refugee Resettlement (ORR, 1994: 54-64; ORR,1995, pp. 54-67) the labor force participation rates and employment to population ratios (EPR[2]) of Southeast Asian refugees have been considerably different from those of other ethnic or nationality groups of refugees resettled in the United States. Comparing the average labor force participation rate (43.6 percent) and EPR (35.4 percent) for all refugees who arrived between 1989 and 1994, Southeast Asian refugees who arrived during the same period are lower (36.4 percent and 34.9 percent for Vietnamese labor force participation rates and EPR, respectively; 20.2 percent and 11.7 percent for other Southeast Asian refugees' labor force participation rate and EPR, respectively). More specifically, among several ethnic or nationality groups, Vietnamese and other Southeast Asian refugees have the lowest labor force status: refugees from Latin America (71.2 percent and 57.0 percent), Eastern Europe (61.0 percent and 52.9 percent), Africa (55.0 percent and 39.6 percent), former Soviet Union (51.1 percent and 35.9 percent), and Middle East (39.4 percent and 23.6 percent) all have higher participation rates than Southeast Asian refugees.

Table 1.1: Labor force status and the use of public assistance of selected refugee groups   unit: %

	Viet-nam	Oth-er SEA	Afr-ica	Latin Ame-rica	Mid-dle East	East-ern Eur-ope	Soviet	All
LFPR	36.4	20.2	55.0	71.2	39.4	61.0	51.1	43.6
ERR	34.9	11.7	39.6	57.0	23.6	52.9	35.9	35.4
CA	58.1	84.8	35.7	14.7	65.6	15.9	54.8	53.5

LFPR: Labor Force Participation Rate.
ERP: Employment-to-Population Ratio.
The Cash Assistance(CA) includes AFDC, Refuge Cash Assistance (RCA), SSI, and General Assistance(GA).
Source: Office of Refugee Resettlement (1995, p. 56, 64).

As reviewed above and as already pointed out by many prior studies (Potocky and McDonald, 1995), even among Southeast Asian refugees, there is an ethnic difference in the labor force status of Vietnamese and other Southeast Asian refugees. Not surprisingly, lower labor force status for Southeast Asian refugees results in more extensive use of public assistance. Group differences between Southeast Asian refugees and other refugees, and Vietnamese and other Southeast Asian refugees are also evident in use of public assistance as shown in table 1.1. Among all refugee cohorts arrived in the U.S. between 1989 and 1994, Vietnamese and other Southeast Asian refugees use public assistance most extensively. On average 53.5 percent of all refugees use at least one kind of public assistance. The rates for Vietnamese refugees and other Southeast Asian refugees are about 58 percent and 85 percent, respectively, as of October 1994. Public assistance utilization for Southeast Asian refugees is dramatically higher than that for Latin American (14.7 percent), Eastern European (15.9 percent), and African (35.7 percent) refugees. Only rates for refugees from the former Soviet Union (54.8 percent) and Middle East (65.6 percent) approach those for Vietnamese or other Southeast Asian refugees.

More striking is public assistance utilization rates of Southeast Asian refugee households by the length of residence in the United States. In general, non-SEA refugee households are likely to exit gradually from welfare dependency over time (within the initial 5 years after arrival). That is, the percent of households which depend only on public assistance for their living decreases from about 41 to about 21 and the percent of households which depend only on their earnings increases rapidly from about 20 to 53 during the initial 5 years of resettlement. In contrast, the welfare dependence rate for Southeast Asian refugee households increases from about 35 percent to 50 percent over time. Similarly, fewer Southeast Asian refugee households achieve self-sufficiency although the percent of self-sufficient households doubled in the same five-year period (ORR, 1995, p. 62). Based on these features of Southeast Asian refugees' economic and labor force status, it is not difficult to conclude that high rates of poverty prevail among them although there is no empirical study about this cohort.

Despite the economic hardship experienced by Southeast Asian refugees or refugee households, historically little research has focused on issues related to their experience in the process of resettlement in the U.S. or on ways to enhance their labor force participation and economic status. In part, this may be due to the recent arrival of Southeast Asian refugees to the United States. in first half of this decade. Except for Annual Reports by the ORR, which present basic statistics about the Southeast Asian refugees' economic adjustment, little is known about their resettlement experience.

Also, most studies of Southeast Asian refugees concentrate on examining the relationship between individual refugees' characteristics and their economic or labor force status (Bach and Caroll-Seguin, 1986; Gordon, 1988; Kim, 1989; Lee and Edmonston, 1994; Majka and Mullen, 1992; Rumbaut, 1989). However, research based on individual refugees is not sufficient to lead us to a more comprehensive understanding of the refugee resettlement experience and the most appropriate policy and practice implications for resettlement services. This argument is based on the belief that an individual's economic well-being depends generally on the whole household economy and, accordingly, that individual refugees' labor force or economic status must be examined in the family or household context. For the Southeast Asian refugee population, analyses of labor force status at the household level seems to be especially relevant given emphasis among this ethnic group on strong family ties (Haines, 1988) and the importance of family collectivism on economic resource arrangements (Kibria, 1994).

This study also argues against the existing household-level studies of the Southeast Asian refugee population. Previous studies analyzing households as units of analysis, in addition to analyses of individuals, have aimed to identify the significant predictors for economic outcomes in Southeast Asian refugee households such as household income, the use of public assistance, or poverty status (Caplan, Whitmore, and Bui, 1985; Potocky and McDonald, 1995). Although these studies do make a contribution toward explaining economic hardship in Southeast Asian refugee households, in order to reveal the family or household dynamics in income generation, it is necessary to focus on household income generation activities such as the participation in the labor force, employment, or the quality of employment of household members as well as the outcomes mentioned above.

Household-level study for the labor force status of refugee population fits well with the current direction of refugee service policy, which emphasizes the family rather than the individual as a unit of self-sufficiency. Furthermore, multiple-earner strategies are increasingly recommended as a model of self-sufficiency and economic adjustment of refugee households which states and voluntary agencies can adopt for their entire programs to foster family or household self-sufficiency (ORR, 1995, p. 71).

However, this policy directive has not been based on empirical evidence from the study of factors that generate of multiple earners in refugee households, particularly in the Southeast Asian refugee household. This means that the topic of multiple-earner strategies has not been discussed in the research on refugee resettlement experience in the United States. A great deal more needs to be learned in order to support the policy objectives. For example: Who are the important wage-earners in the SEA household ?; What is the prevailing composition of wage-earners in Southeast Asian refugee households?; What demographic and human capital factors are associated with the presence of multiple earners in the Southeast Asian refugee household?

OBJECTIVES OF THIS BOOK

The objectives for this book can be largely divided into two parts. One major objective is to expand our understanding about household mechanisms in the generation of wage labor among Southeast Asian refugee households in the early resettlement phase. The other objective is to offer policy and practice implications for refugee resettlement services in the United States.

The first objective can be subdivided into two components for research purposes: to analyze the wage-labor composition of Southeast Asian refugee households and to explore the significant factors which differentiate multiple-earner households from nonmultiple-earner households among Southeast Asian refugee households. Analyses of wage-labor composition in the household concentrate on revealing the labor force status of household members classified by their family status and the distribution of wage-earners among refugee households. Also, this study examines whether the labor force status of household members and the distributions of wage-earners vary close different cohorts, including ethnicity, location of resettlement (by states), and the type of household (e.g., nuclear, extended, singles, etc.). Another important objective in this section is to determine if there is a unique composition of household members for pooling of wage-labor in the Southeast Asian refugee household, which is different from a conventional model of multiple wage-earners in general American family households (e.g. husband-wife dual earner strategy).

Along with the analyses of household wage-earner composition, a search for important factors which are associated with multiple wage-earners in Southeast Asian refugee household is intended to provide significant policy and practice implication for planning and delivering resettlement services for refugees in the early resettlement period. Many refugee resettlement services are aimed at generating wage labor and encouraging economic self-sufficiency. The findings from analyses examining the composition of wage-earners in Southeast Asian refugee households and significant factors associated with the presence of multiple-earners will provide useful information for refugee assistance policy and practice.

RESEARCH QUESTIONS

This book aims to address the following important question: what are the factors associated with the use of multiple wage-earner strategies among Southeast Asian refugee households in the early resettlement period (less than 5 years of residing in the United States)?

In this research the multiple earner strategy of a refugee household means: efforts by a household to overcome economic difficulty caused primarily by individual refugees' labor market disadvantages (particularly that of the household head) by sending more than one household member to the labor market. Under the broad research question of the study and the concept of multiple earner strategy, this book pursues two specific research questions: 1) what is the prevailing composition of multiple wage-earners in the Southeast Asian refugee household during the initial 5 years of resettlement in the U.S.? ; and 2) what factors are significant in differentiating the SEA refugee households which contain multiple wage-earners from other Southeast Asian refugee households ?

To answer the first research question, several more fundamental research questions are asked.

1. What characteristics of household structure, household-level human capital, and environmental factors are related to the experience of Southeast Asian refugee household members? How are these characteristics different according to the ethnicity of the household members, in particular, between Vietnamese and non-Vietnamese households?

2. What is the household composition in terms of family status of household members (i.e., the household head, the spouse of the head, adult children of the head, and other families and

relatives) and what is their labor force status and wage incomes? Specifically, what is the labor force status of the household head and of non-head household members? How are the answers for this second question different according to different household composition types (e.g., nuclear, extended, etc.)?

3. What are the distributions of the number of wage-earners among Southeast Asian refugee households? What is the proportion of households which generate multiple wage-earners, households which can generate only one wage-earner, and households which have no earner? And, what is the meaning of multiple-earners among Southeast Asian refugee households in terms of household wage income, welfare receipts, and poverty status? How do these indices change for a Southeast Asian refugee household with an increase in the number of wage-earners?

4. What is the prevailing composition of household members for multiple wage-earners in Southeast Asian refugee households? Who are wage- earners in the household, apart from the household heads? Are these compositions different with the household type, ethnicity, and other applicable classification criteria?

These questions are for the purpose of presenting the distribution of family status in a household and the economic contribution to a household of a household head and other earners and examining whether there are unique features of the household wage labor composition, which could differ from the conventional model of multiple-earners in American households.

For the second important research question, "what are the significant factors that explain variation in the presence of multiple wage-earners," the present study draws on variables in three domains: household structure, human capital of household level, and environmental factors related to SEA refugee resettlement in the United States. These variables are discussed more extensively in the next chapters.

Since the major research focus is on factors associated with multiple wage-earners in Southeast Asian refugee households, it may miss differences between the households which have none or only one wage-earner and between the households which have one and those with multiple wage-earners in a household. Therefore, this study will also consider the significant factors associated with transitions in the number of wage-earners (i.e., from none to one wage-earner in a household and from one to multiple wage-earners in a household).

REFUGEE ASSISTANCE PROGRAMS IN THE UNITED STATES

Although this book concentrates more on refugee family's strategies for economic adaptation than on refugee assistance programs, a brief explanation about the programs helps readers understand the content of this study.

Refugee assistance programs in the United States. can be divided into three primary roles: admissions of refugees, reception and placement activities, and refugee resettlement programs (ORR, 1994). The admission process involves the selection of entrants from the refugee applicants based on the Refugee Act of 1980 and the distribution of refugees in states. The reception and placement process includes activities related to the initial placement of refugees such as pre-arrival service (identifying relatives, selecting an agency which will help the refugees, and developing travel arrangements), reception ("initial housing, furnishings, food and clothing for a minimum of 30 days"), and counseling and referrals (orienting the refugees to the community and informing them about health, employment, and training). These initial reception and placement activities are carried out by voluntary non-profit agencies "through cooperative agreements with the Bureau of Population, Refugees, and Migration of the Department of State" (ORR, 1995, p. 11). Finally, the refugee resettlement programs, a primary part of the refugee assistance process, consist of various state-administered refugee assistance programs including cash, medical and social services, and special projects.

Cash and medical assistance include AFDC, SSI, and Medicaid for the individuals or family members who qualify for the benefits on the same basis as U.S. citizens. Refugees who are not eligible for those benefits but are needy may receive Refuge Cash Assistance (RCA) and Refugee Medical Assistance (RMA). General Assistance (GA) and General Medical Assistance (GMA) are established for the needy refugees who are not eligible for AFDC, SSI and Medicaid and also no longer eligible for RCA and RMA. "In States with GA or GMA, refugees are eligible to the same extent as non-refugee residents of the State" (ORR, 1994, p. 17). In addition, refugees may be eligible to receive food stamps on the same basis as non-refugee residents.

Prior to FY 1981, most of the state-administered programs were fully reimbursed by federal funds. However, since 1981 the reimbursements by the federal government have rapidly decreased. In the early 1980s, refugee programs performed by states were reimbursed for up to a maximum of 18-36 months after arrival. As of 1993, the federal funds for reimbursements of state programs are only for RCA and RMA for the first 8 months after arrival.

The federal government's policies stress social services "especially to promote rapid achievement of self-sufficiency" (ORR, 1995, p. 24), which are called "priority services" The social service programs for refugees include "employment service, English language training, vocational training, and other support services to promote economic self-sufficiency and reduce refugee dependence on public assistance programs" (ORR, 1994, p. 12). Other targeted and alternative programs such as discretionary programs of the federal government (Office of Refugee Resettlement) also assist refugees in terms of employment and other social support.

The funds for resettlement services are allocated by the Office of Refugee Resettlement to the states in accordance with refugee admission numbers. State governments contract with local entities for actual resettlement service delivery. Therefore, actual refugee resettlement services are delivered by local entities, which represent, in general, "private, nonprofit organizations under the purview of religious entities" (Le-Doux and Stephens, 1992, p. 34). Nationally, approximately 12-13 large agencies are serving refugees. The three largest voluntary agencies are the United States Catholic Conference, the YMCA, and the Church World Service (Le-Doux and Stephens, 1992).

NOTES

1. These concerns were already for the immigrants under the changed immigration regulation for entry from the quarter system to entry based on family unification. The recent immigrants, especially from the third world, have been the object of the same concerns from the public as for refugees.

2. The Employment-to-Population Ratio (EPR) is "the ratio of the number of individuals age 16 or over who are employed (full- or part- time) to the total number of individuals in the population who are age 16 or over" (ORR, 1995:55).

CHAPTER 2

Theoretical and Empirical Backgrounds

MULTIPLE EARNER STRATEGIES AND HOUSEHOLD STRUCTURE

While discussing the concept of family adaptive strategies, Moen and Wethington point out that the family strategies can be described as "the actions families devise for coping with, if not overcoming, the challenges of living, and for achieving their goals in the face of structural barriers" (1992, p. 234). When the goal is economic well-being, for instance, "families as collective entities send their members out to work, assign household tasks, share wages and resources, [etc.]" (Moen and Wethington, 1992, p. 235).

Focusing on the arrangement of wage labor in the family, if the income of the head of the household is not enough to meet "a desired standard of living" or sometimes, to meet even basic economic needs, other family or household members, for instance, a spouse, adult children, and other relatives, tend to participate in the labor force to obtain more income for the household (Mincer, 1960). Dual earners (i.e., husband and wife) in low income American households can be an example. According to a recent study about work and family, "the pressure to opt for the first solution [i.e., two wage earners in the family] may have been especially great in recent decades when real wages, contrary to historical trends, have been declining" (Ferber and O'Farrell, 1991, p. 30). The pressure to work has greatly increased for the wives since "the families of men in low-income occupations are in greater need of more income" (Ferber and O'Farrell, 1991, p. 30).

The pooling of wage labor in a household has frequently been stressed as a very important economic resource for immigrant economic adjustment in the United States. (Angel and Tienda, 1982; Jensen, 1991; Perez, 1986)

Jensen (1991), studying the ability of secondary earners (family earners other than the head) to lift families out of poverty, compared immigrant and native families and suggested that the impact of poverty amelioration by secondary earners is greater for immigrant than native families. More importantly, Jensen used logistic regression for the multivariate analyses to predict the probability of escaping poverty among those families that dip below the poverty level when the earnings of secondary earners are subtracted from the total family income. Jensen, for the regression analysis, examined the role of several independent variables from three domains: individual, family, and contextual variables. The results indicate that, among recent immigrant families, the advantage from secondary earners is "explained by their greater propensity to be headed by married couples, to be extended, and to live outside the South and metropolitan areas" (Jensen, 1991, p. 137). However, such characteristics of an individual as a household head's age and education were not significant as a predictor for immigrant households' economic improvement by the contribution of secondary earners.

The research of Jensen, as he stresses, is driven by the theme that "the spread of work across family members is an important strategy for making up income shortfalls" (p. 114). In other words, a full utilization of household labor force potential is believed to be a very effective battle against family poverty (Jensen, 1991).

Perez (1986) also emphasizes the importance of family organization in the successful economic adjustment of Cuban immigrants in the United States. She argues that consideration of the economic organization of the family, which facilitates upward social mobility, can bridge an individual approach (such as focusing on human capital characteristics) and a structural one (such as focusing on community or ethnic economic enclaves) and accordingly provides a more comprehensive understanding of immigrant economic adjustment than the individual and the structural approach.

In her study, while pointing out that the family income of Cuban immigrants is closer to that of U.S. families than other Spanish-origin families in the U.S. are to the U.S. average, Perez suggests that "Cubans' comparatively high family income is largely not the result of relatively high individual income" but the result of different household economic strategies, that is, "proportionately more workers per family than both the Hispanic and U.S. populations" (1986, p. 10). In other words, Cuban immigrant families were more likely to have two or more workers than the other two populations. As interrelated characteristics to the relatively higher number of workers among Cuban families, Perez suggested such factors as high rates of female labor force participation, low fertility of women, and the economic contribution of the elderly. The most obvious way that the elderly can contribute to the economic welfare of the family is "to serve as caretakers for their grandchildren, thereby facilitating the employment of their daughter or daughter-in-law" (Perez, 1986, p.14).

Angel and Tienda (1982) examined the relationship between household composition and sources of household income among Hispanics, blacks, and non-Hispanic whites and found that nonnuclear family members (family members other than the head, spouse, and adult children) in black and Hispanic extended family households contribute significantly to total household income. The nonnuclear members' contribution "may also serve as a compensatory strategy for supplementing the temporarily or chronically low earnings of minority household heads" (Angel and Tienda, 1982, p.1360). They also commented that "the fact that some minority households have incomes below the poverty level in spite of the supplemental income of nonnuclear members indicates that the economic contributions of nonnuclear members do not offset the labor market disadvantages faced by minority heads" (Angel and Tienda, 1982, p. 1380).

Women's economic activity has also been discussed as an issue for multiple-earner strategy. The literature on this issue discusses income and wage offers, education of adult women in a household, the number and ages of children in a household, and household structure as typical factors for married women's labor market behavior. However, the prime concern in this area is the relationship between child care duty or costs and the participation of mothers in the labor force (Blau and Robins, 1989; Floge, 1989; Tienda and Glass, 1985; Wong and Levine, 1992).

Tienda and Glass (1985) found that the presence of female nuclear adults such as adult daughters is a very important factor to increase the probability of labor force participation among American mothers who were heads of households. Other studies, in general, note that child care availability (in and outside of home) was positively associated with labor force participation by the mothers (Blau and Robins, 1989).

Wong and Levine (1992), in multivariate analyses of young married women (15-49 years old) who had given birth within the last five years and who were living in urban Mexico, suggest that the mothers with higher potential wage offers, with a potential care taker in the household and with a less well-educated husband, are more likely to work. They also found that the "mothers with fewer children ages 6-12 years, and with more children above age 13, are more likely to be employed" (p. 97).

The studies presented above are very significant for the SEA refugee population in the United States. In general, refugee household heads are expected to be similar to those of immigrant households in that they are more likely to be unemployed or to bring insufficient income into the household than their counterparts among U.S. households. The economic disadvantages of immigrant household heads are often explained by the lack of skills or occupational knowledge which can be accepted in the country of destination,[1] (Chiswick, 1979) and this situation is not limited to household heads but is the same for most household members who want to participate in the labor market. For household heads and other adult household members who are involuntary international migrants, the difficulty is expected to be equal to or more than that for heads among voluntary international migrant households (Gold, 1988; Waldinger, 1984). Furthermore, for the refugees in the initial period of resettlement, this difficulty is expected to be more serious than for their predecessors. Facing economic difficulty resulting from the household head's insufficient income, other household members' participation in the labor force is to be encouraged.

HOUSEHOLD APPROACH IN SEA REFUGEE POPULATION

Compared to the volume of documents on Southeast Asian refugees' economic adjustment in the United States, the studies which discuss wage labor composition in the refugee family or household are few. Analyzing data from the 1982 survey for 1384 Southeast Asian refugee households, Caplan, Whitmore, and Bui (1985) report that as the number of jobs per household increases a household is more likely to be above the poverty level. According to their study, while 83 percent of the households with no earner and 32 percent of the households with one earner were below the poverty level, only 7 percent of the households with two or more earners were in the same situation. They also examined the relationship between the household type and economic status of households and found that extended families (43 percent) and multiple families (40 percent) were less likely to fall below the poverty level than nuclear families (61 percent). When households contained unrelated single(s) or when households consisted only of single(s), their economic status compared to the poverty line appeared to be considerably better than the households without the single(s). Therefore, reporting the factor of "the presence of unrelated and presumably employable singles in a households" as a substantively effective one, the authors stress that "household composition arrangement is a real boon to immediate self-sufficiency" (Caplan et al., 1985, p. 202).

Haines (1988) stresses that "the availability of increased numbers and proportions of adult wage-earners is key to the economic success of refugees in the United States" (p. 11) and that this sort of multiple wage-earner strategy can be well applied to Vietnamese refugee households because their intrinsic structure of traditional kinship can make an additional wage-earner available within the household.

He also discusses the points suggested by Caplan and his associates. "If it is nuclear family households that appear to be in the most difficulty, and a difficulty statistically ameliorated when they add an additional (and potentially employable) member, then dual working parent model [i.e., husband-and-wife model] is indeed not the entire issue—even though Vietnamese female labor force participation rates are relatively high" (Haines, 1988, p. 8). Therefore, Haines recommended that we must consider the structural complexity of Vietnamese households and the "broader array of individuals who can be in the secondary or supplemental income-generating role" (p. 8) instead of the simple application of an existing model to the population. He detailed this issue by presenting a specific feature of Vietnamese kinship from a previous survey[2]: the considerable proportion of adult children (male and female adults categorized as the child or spouse of the child of the household head among all male adults and all female adults, respectively). These child-adults, whose English language competence might be greater than that of their parents, "along with siblings, other relatives, and other single adults, represent key resources available to the household in its quest for successful economic adjustment" and can be a basic structural feature of Vietnamese kinship, which "provide quite specific options and mechanisms for such economic adjustment" (Haines, 1988, p. 9).

A recent ethnographic study (Kibria, 1994) provides a quite detailed elaboration of the household composition, internal family relations, and social contexts. Kibria (1994), from a study of newly arrived Vietnamese refugees in Philadelphia, emphasizes that a particular household and family organization, that is, "age and gender heterogeneity" is a helpful factor in the economic life of Vietnamese refugee households along with family ideology such as family collectivism, which encourages cooperative economic behavior for all household members, including children. A household in which the age and gender of household members are diverse, is likely to be "hierarchical in its internal relations" and "such a household, in which some members have substantial authority over others, may organize its economic activities quite differently than a household that is homogeneous and thus egalitarian in its relations between members" (Kibria, 1994, p. 93). Kibria notes that "hierarchical households may be better able to demand economic behavior from members that calls for self-sacrifice and is directed towards familial rather than individual goals" (p. 93).

Also, the age and gender diversity in family organization can be considered as an economic advantage due to the "specific character of the structural environment that surrounded them" (Kibria, 1994, p. 93), for example, the presence of governmental aid and services (e.g., cash and medical assistance, and public schooling). These programs and services mean the sources of the economic contributions to the household, which are economically valued resources not for only "a particular age and gender group (for example, young men) but generally for young or elderly household members"(Kibria, 1994, p. 93).

The prior documents reviewed here provide a basic framework for the present study. However, none seem to illustrate the household or family mechanism in organizing wage labor as a process of refugee resettlement. In contrast, some of them present details which are beyond the coverage of this present study. For example, Kibria (1994) touched on matters of family ideology such as collectivism and hierarchical structure possibly internalized in the Southeast Asian refugee households, and other kinds of economic resources that non-wage earners can bring into the households, such as the benefits of government aid programs. Although these aspects can be important factors for the economic adjustment of Southeast Asian refugee households, the present study does not include those aspects because this study concentrates on wage labor as a fundamental criterion for economic adjustment and because the data that this study is based on does not permit the information about internal family relations Kibria discussed.

The labor force status of Southeast Asian refugee women also needs to be considered in the context of the pooling of wage labor in the household. Particularly, examination of the labor force participation and employment of wives among Southeast Asian refugees can be a significant index to determine if the dual-earner model (typically husband-wife) among American family households extends to Southeast Asian refugee households or, otherwise, if Southeast Asian refugee households maintain different structures of wage labor pooling.

Most prior studies of Southeast Asian refugee women compared the labor force or economic status of the women with those of Southeast Asian refugee men. Bach and Carroll-Seguin (1986), by using labor statistics from 1982 and 1983, found that Southeast Asian refugee women participate in the labor force at a rate more than 15 percent below their male counterparts. In the logistic regression analysis, they also found that Southeast Asian refugee women were less likely to be in the labor force by 15 percent than males when other conditions were controlled (Bach and Carroll-Seguin, 1986). However, the labor force participation of the refugee men was also constrained by child care responsibility to a similar extent and the constraint for men by the presence of children at home was triple that of the latest cohort (arrivals from 1980 to 1983) than the earliest cohort (arrivals from 1975 to 1979). For these surprising findings, they suggest an explanation. The household strategy of wage income generation is perhaps less gender specific in the earliest years of resettlement. "The important goal is to get whoever can obtain a job into the labor force. In many cases, female refugees have an easier time finding an entry-level job" (Bach and Carroll-Seguin, 1986, p. 398). Accordingly, "the anticipated gender specific effect of child care responsibilities may be diminished" (Bach and Carroll-Seguin, 1988, p. 398). They also suggest that "child care responsibilities may be more shared among men and women" (Bach and Carroll-Seguin, 1988, p. 399) in the Southeast Asian refugee population than we expected compared to the general U.S. population.

Household type can be a significant factor in generating wage labor when the gender of Southeast Asian refugees is controlled. Bach and Carroll-Seguin found (1988) that only women can benefit from the extended household structure in their labor force participation.

HUMAN CAPITAL AND SOUTHEAST ASIAN REFUGEE HOUSEHOLDS

Human capital represents "the stock of economically productive human capabilities" (Greenwald, 1994, p. 493) such as knowledge and skills embodied in people. These human capabilities can be developed by investments in human beings. Examples of human capital investments are expenditures on education, training, and emotional and physical health (Becker, 1993, p. 54). Human capital theorists emphasize the rate of return on human capital investment, which can be calculated by comparing the earnings stream in discounted value on alternative courses of actions (Becker, 1993; Rosen, 1987) and have investigated and observed the relationship between schooling, earnings, and family background (Rosen, 1987).

These theoretical concepts and empirical findings have provided an important explanation for the distribution of income and earnings among people and the matter of poverty (Rosen, 1987). Policy implications of the theoretical approach traditionally have primarily been in education and training for the unemployed and socially and economically disadvantaged, including the poor, welfare recipients, teen-aged youth, older workers who lack skills, and dislocated workers. Historically, various kinds of education and training programs initiated by the federal government such as, the Manpower Development and Training Act (MDTA), Economic Opportunity Act (EOA), the Comprehensive Employment and Training Act (CETA) and the Job Training Partnership Act (JTPA), are reflections of the belief that investment in education and training empowers people in employment. In general, those programs offer occupational training in classrooms or on-the-job, remedial education before skill training, adult basic education and English training, job creation, and employability development programs like employment counseling, career assessment, and allowance for transportation (Marshall and Briggs, 1989).

The core of human resources development programs for refugees, that is, general education, job skills training, and employability development, can be found in refugee resettlement services. The social services initiated by a state, which take the second largest budget for the resettlement programs (the first one is cash and medical assistance) consist of English language training, job training, and other employment development services (ORR,1990).

This book, along with the variables of household structure and environments, examines the effects of human capital and investment in human capital on the generation of multiple earners in the Southeast Asian refugee households. Selected variables of human capital are education in the home country, the length of English language instruction and job training, English language fluency, health condition (mental and physical), the length of residence in the United States, and the age of adult household members who are 16 or older, except high school students.

Age is regarded as a kind of human capital because it can reflect years of experience. According to Tigges (1988), "aging represents the contradictory forces of accumulation of experience and decline in physical strength and stamina" (Tigges, 1988, p. 678). That is, as the accumulation of experience continues through retraining or updating skills, return to the human capital investment increases with age. However, at a certain age (in general, after middle age), physical decline "offsets the value of accumulated experience, bringing wages down for older workers relative to middle-aged workers" (Tigges, 1988, p. 678). In general, the age-earnings profile based on cross-sectional data is known to be a convex curve (Stolzenberg, 1975).

When the labor force participation of Southeast Asian refugees was examined by the age variable, the adults less than 25 years old and over 45 years old fared were disadvantageous compared to those who were in the remaining ages (25-45) (Bach and Carroll-Seguin, 1986; Majka and Mullan, 1992). These "refugee-specific age patterns for labor force entrance and over all employment are similar to those for the U.S. population" (Majka and Mullan, 1992, p. 903). On the other hand, the results of another study (Rumbaut, 1989) indicate that age has a weak but negative effect on the level of earnings. That is, "the older the refugee, the lower the level of earnings" (Rumbaut, 1989, p. 162).

This study classifies the household variables related to age, mean age of adult household members in the household, and the percentage of adult household members who were in a certain age category (i.e., 25-55 for so-called prime age range) as factors of human capital.

The length of residence in the U.S. was included in the category of human capital in this study because this factor was believed to also reflect the accumulation of experience. We may expect that, "as time goes on, refugees pick up English skills, learn the cultural mazeways, [and] cut into friendship networks which help to find employment" (Caplan et al., 1985, p. 210). In general, it is known that the longer refugees reside in the U.S., the higher economic or labor force status they achieve (Caplan et al., 1985; ORR, 1994; Potocky and McDonald, 1995).

Many prior studies of the resettlement and economic adjustment of SEA refugees examined the relationship between their human capital and economic or labor force status. Bach and Carroll-Seguin (1986) studied the relationship between the years of education in the home country and the rate of labor force participation for Southeast Asian refugees using two cohorts classified by the time of arrival in the US: the first cohort of 1975-1979 and the second of 1980-1983. They found that regardless of the arrival time and sex, the magnitude (.03) of Pearson correlation between the years of schooling and labor force participation was almost consistent. That is "an additional year of former schooling provides a three percentage point advantage over the person without an extra year of training" (Bach and Carroll-Seguin, 1986, p. 398). Another recent study (Lee and Edmonston, 1994), however, revealed a negative relationship between household income and schooling among Vietnamese Americans.

English has been another important issue in the studies of the relationship between human capital investments and the returns for immigrants and refugees (Bach and Carroll-Seguin 1986; Lee and Edmonston, 1994). The Office of Refugee Resettlement also has reported that English language fluency is a very important determinant of weekly wages as well as labor force participation and employment possibility (ORR, 1990). Although there is some deviance from the general trend, English fluency usually increases the labor force participation rate, decreases unemployment possibility, and enhances weekly wages of Southeast Asian refugees (ORR, 1990).

Most of the examined variables of human capital, especially education and English language fluency, are for individual refugees. In this book, however, which is based on the household as an analysis unit, the human capital of all household members in a household will be averaged for each of such kinds of human capital as age, education, English language, health, length of training, etc. Each of these averaged values represents each kind of human capital of a household level, not of an individual refugee. Then, this study examines those kinds of averaged human capital on a household level, along with other independent variables, as potential predictors for the variation in generating multiple earners among Southeast Asian refugee households. This analysis design is based on the assumption that the human capital of a person is not appropriate as a predictor for the economic variation of a household because it can be at best a partial interpretation of the human resources available within a household.

Rodriguez (1992) also points out this issue while finding significant factors for the variation of household income among Puerto Ricans on the U.S. mainland. While examining the householder's characteristics such as age, education, and other demographic variables in the regression model, he commented that "using the characteristics of one person [e.g., a household head] to predict the income pooled by several members of the household can result in difficulties when interpreting the results" (p. 55). Therefore, it would rather be desirable to include shares of all adult household members in the research based on a household as an analysis unit. Transformation of individual household members' values of human capital into household-level value has been witnessed in several studies on SEA refugees (Caplan et al., 1985; Potocky and McDonald, 1995).

Caplan and his associates used the transformed figures (primarily mean figures) of all household members for such variables as age, English proficiency , and education status (from no education to more than college graduation) in their descriptive and multivariate analyses. Receipt of transfer income as a dependent variable was positively related to the average English proficiency of the household at the time of arrival. The dependent variable also had a bimodal relationship to mean age of the household. The bimodal relationship means that "the youngest and the oldest are more likely found on transfer income while those on earned income are more often in the middle age range, i.e., 24-55" (Caplan et al., 1985, p. 199). The other dependent variable, household income below the poverty-level, was strongly related to arrival English proficiency of household members but not significantly related to the education in the home country of household members.

Potocky and McDonald (1995) provided more specific explanations for the variables of aggregated information for the household. While studying Southeast Asian refugees in California, they calculated the average age, average length of residence in the

United States, and average years of education of all people over age 15 in the household. They also aggregated the value of disability (i.e., total number of disabled people in a household) for all household members in a household who were over 15. Finally, to aggregate English proficiency for all household members over age 15, they used a concept of "linguistic isolation" that asks whether a household had any members over age 15 who spoke English very well. Of these factors manipulated for the household-level analyses, the most important predictors for household income were education (positive) for household income.[3] The rest of the independent variables related to human capital had comparatively minor effects on household income. However, the older the household members, the longer they lived in the United States., the more proficient they were in English, and the less likely they were to have disabled person in the household, the higher household income they had.

The effects of health and training programs on the economic and labor force status were not frequently addressed in the prior studies. According to the study by Caplan and his associates, poor health posed a major barrier to economic status, although health problems were not a significant factor for leaving welfare and entering the work force on the personal level (Caplan et al., 1985, p. 218). Their study also examined vocational training related to the economic status of Southeast Asian refugees and found that having received vocational training had a positive relationship with not being on cash assistance and with gaining earned income.

ENVIRONMENTAL FACTORS FOR REFUGEE RESETTLEMENT

In addition to household structure and human capital, this book also includes the variables related to the environment of the refugees and examines the relationship between the environmental factors and the generation of multiple earners. The selected environmental factors for this study are the ethnicity of the household, the first state in which they resettled, the availability of transportation to jobs or training for the household members, and the extent of current participation in education or training for the household members.

The labor market structures and conditions (e.g., segmented labor market, ethnic enclave economy, and employers' attitudes) are frequently discussed as an influential factor of the environments on the economic adjustment of ethnic minorities, immigrants or refugees face (Majka and Mullan, 1992; Portes and Stepick, 1985; Wilson and Portes, 1980; Wooden, 1991). Unfortunately, however, the data used for this paper do not include these kinds of information. Ethnicity of refugees has frequently been identified as an important variable for the labor force and economic status of Southeast Asian refugees. In general, Chinese Vietnamese and Vietnamese refugees fare better than other Southeast Asian ethnic groups (e.g., Hmong, Laotian, and Cambodian) in the employment status (Potocky and McDonald, 1995). Individual refugees among the Vietnamese and Chinese-Vietnamese use public assistance less than the others and those of the first two groups are also higher than the latter in household incomes (Potocky and McDonald, 1995).

The higher labor force status and economic level of Vietnamese individuals and households have been explained by the fact that they came from a more westernized, and urbanized society than did the other ethnic groups (Rumbaut, 1989; Potocky and McDonald, 1994). The social and economic support from the ethnic enclaves established by the earlier arrivals is suggested as another reason for the economic well-being of Vietnamese refugees, an advantage not found among the other ethnic groups (Potocky and McDonald, 1994).

Residence in California for Southeast Asian refugees is considered to be a very negative factor for their labor force status (Bach and Argiros, 1991; Bach and Carroll-Seguin, 1986) and as a facilitator to increase the extent of public assistance use (Bach and Argiros, 1991). The authors suggest several reasons: employment difficulty due to geographical concentration in a few metropolitan areas (i.e., several southern counties in California); class structure or composition of existing ethnic communities; and California's public assistance rules and practices (e.g., higher benefits from the assistance than other states).

This book also includes such factors as availability of transportation and current enrollment in language or training programs or in schools except high schools for Southeast Asian household members as expected predictors for the generation of multiple earners.

DEFINITION OF TERMS

Household and family. Officially "a family is defined as two or more persons living together who are related by blood, marriage, or adoption" and "a household is defined as one or more persons living in the same dwelling unit and sharing living expenses" (Ferber and O'Farrell, 1991, p. 26). Therefore, "all families are households, but all households are not families" (Ferber and O'Farrell, 1991, p. 26). However, since all of the household members in the data analyzed for this study are related by family ties, we can use the terms "family" and "household" interchangeably in this book.

Household member is defined in the data as "every person who lives in the residence (i.e., home), or who is staying or visiting the residence and has no other home" (Please refer to page 4 of Questionnaire for Annual Survey of Refugees given in Appendix.)

Labor force participation is defined as being employed a week before the survey date or looking for a job during the four weeks previous to the time of survey.

EPR (Employment-to-Population Ratio) is the ratio of the number of individuals age 16 or over who are employed (full-or part-time) to the total number of individuals in the population who are age 16 or over. It is called 'employment rate' (ORR, 1995).

Household income includes every kind of earned income and transferred income such as public assistance and other cash assistance acquired by all household members.

The definitions of the *household types* follow the ones of Caplan and his associates (Caplan et al., 1985, p. 51) except for the definition of the nuclear family. Their definition of nuclear family household members includes possibly one grandparent in addition to the compositions of a husband and a wife or parent(s) and child(ren). However, the presence of one grandparent in the household is believed to be a component for extended household (Wagner, 1995). Therefore, this book employs the definition for a nuclear family used in the study of Angel and Tienda (1982)—a head, spouse, and one or more own children.[4]

Nuclear Family—the household that has one of the following compositions
        Husband and wife
        Parent (s) and child (ren)

Extended Family—combination of nuclear family + others related by blood or marriage or a household of relatives without a nuclear family being present.

Multiple family—any combination of unrelated second parent/child or husband/wife or any combination of unrelated + extended relatives

Single(s)—Unrelated single individual(s)

Head of household is defined as "the person in whose name [a residence] is rented, owned, or is being bought" (Refer to page 4 of Questionnaire for Annual Survey of Refugees given in Appendix.)

The poverty thresholds follow the federal poverty thresholds that were originally developed by the Social Security Administration for statistical purposes. The thresholds vary by family size and have been updated by the percentage change in the Consumer Price Index for All Urban Consumers (CPI-U) (SSA, 1993).

NOTES

1. Chiswick (1979) called this situation 'lack of skill transferability.' The skill transferability represents the extent to which skills acquired in the country of origin can be accepted and used in the country of destination. At the time of arrival, "immigrants from countries with a language, culture, technology, and economic and legal structure similar to that in their destination would find their skills more readily transferable than those from countries with greater differences" (Chiswick, 1979, p. 358).

2. The source of the data was "Ninth Wave Report: Indochinese Resettlement Operational Feedback," published by OSI (Opportunity Systems, Incorporated) in 1981.

3. The authors also conducted logistic regressions based on individual refugees over age 15 for two dichotomous dependent variables: employment and the use of public assistance.

4. When a household head is a son or a daughter instead of a father or a mother, this type of household is still considered a nuclear family composition unless the adult children are married.

CHAPTER 3

Research Methodology of the Study

SAMPLING AND DATA COLLECTION[1]

This study uses a data set from the Office of Refugee Resettlement (ORR) Annual Survey conducted via telephone interviews in the fall of 1994, by which information on all household members in 1754 refugee households was collected. The Office of Refugee Resettlement's contractor, Arrington Dixon and Associates, Inc., contacted the family by letters in English and in the refugee's native language and interviewed one selected household member in the refugee's native language. If the selected person was a child, an adult living in the same household was interviewed.

The sample was randomly selected from the ORR master data file of refugees who arrived in the U.S. between May 1, 1989 and April 30, 1994. Among these sample refugees, those who arrived between May 1, 1988 and April 30, 1993 were interviewed in the fall of 1993. For the 1994 survey, the refugees who were interviewed for the 1993 survey and had not yet resided in the United States for five years as of April 30, 1994 were re-contacted along with a new sample of the refugees, Amerasians, and entrants who had arrived between May 1, 1989 and April 30, 1994. These cases numbered 1607. Among these cases, only 990 refugees were re-interviewed because of refusal to be interviewed or of not being traced in time to be re-interviewed. On the other hand, among the 936 sample refugees selected from the cohort of newly arrived refugees, only 761 were contacted and interviewed due to the same reasons. Due to the discrepancy between the selected sample and the actual cases interviewed, the data collected were weighted according to year of entry and ethnic group (ORR, 1995, p. 67).

Among all refugee households sampled, 677 are comprised of Southeast Asian refugee households. Among these Southeast Asian refugee households, 577 are Vietnamese households while the remaining 100 comprise other SEA ethnic groups[2]. The 677 Southeast Asian refugee households contain 3510 household members.[3]

DATA DESCRIPTION

The questionnaire for the annual survey of refugees can be divided into two parts.

The first part of the questionnaire collects information about all household members including 1) demographic information and educational and employment background prior to arrival, 2) information on English ability and education, job training, and other education for a degree since they arrived in the United States, 3) information on employment, wages, and income since they arrived in the United States, 4) information on their residence and immigrant status, and 5) health condition related to work and means of handling health care costs.

The second part primarily concerns the use of public aid such as food stamps, AFDC, SSI, Refugee Cash Assistance (RCA), General Assistance (GA), and other cash assistance. Among the public aid mentioned above, RCA, GA, and other cash assistance from refugee assistance agencies, sponsors, or organizations are for refugees only. Also, in this second part, questions are included about other income sources on a regular basis such as interest from saving accounts, net rental income, child support, unemployment compensation or retirement income. Unlike the first part of the questionnaire, which is based on information about every household member, the questions for the second part are asked on the basis of a household.

Thus, the first part of the questionnaire provides information on any given household member while the second represents a household. The given I.D. numbers for the first part and for the second make it possible to connect the two parts and accordingly to match household members to their household.

RESEARCH DESIGN

The research design of this study is a secondary analysis method using existing cross-sectional data. The data has been collected through annual surveys of the Office of Refugee Resettlement of the U.S. Department of Health and Human Services for the purpose of annually reporting to Congress the current situation of the refugees' adjustment process, including language and vocational training participation, labor force participation, employment, and the use of public assistance. The "Report to the Congress," published annually by the Office of Refugee Resettlement, contains the basic statistics consisting primarily of frequencies and crosstabulations to present the trends of labor force participation rates, employment and unemployment rates, and the rate of the use of public assistance. Those indices have been compared by ethnicity or nationality, years of entrance, and other selected factors.

This data set was chosen because it contains demographic information about all household members with their family relations to the household head and detailed information on the labor force status of the household members those who were 16 or older at the time of interview. The information of family relation is essential to analyze the strategies of family wage labor generation and to create household-level human capital and other related variables. Another reason for selecting the data is that they provide up-to-date information about the recently arrived cohort of Southeast Asian refugees, who entered between 1989 and 1994.

Most of variables used in this study were the ones created by transforming the original variables in the data set to the household level. The analysis unit for this study is primarily the household although refugee individuals are analyzed sometimes as those needed. Therefore, the statistics generated for this book rarely duplicate reported in official documents (i.e., Annual Report to Congress).

MEASUREMENT

As mentioned earlier, the major purpose of this book is to find significant factors and their relative importance in the generation of multiple earners. The generation of multiple earners in a Southeast Asian refugee household is expected to be determined by the factors of three large categories: household structure, human capital of household level, and environmental factors. The dependent variables and independent variables represent household-level indicators.

Dependent variable

The dependent variable of this study is based on the number of wage-earners in the household. However, the dependent variable is categorical, such as whether or not there are at least two wage-earners in the household. Therefore, the values of the dependent variable are dichotomous: presence of multiple wage-earners and absence of the earners in the household. This dependent variable is measured by the question presented below, asked of all household members who were 16 or older.

("Did you (or he or she) work at a job anytime last week?" Yes (1) or No (0)

The responses of all adult household members were aggregated and the number of adult household members who were working was used for classifying multiple-earner households. If the total number of adult household members is two or more, the household can be regarded as multiple-earner household. Otherwise, if a household has no or only one worker last week, the household is not a multiple-earner household.

Because the original question did not clarify kinds of work, some of the responses may include self-employed. However, the magnitude of self-employment of all responses was so small (0.9 %, n = 8) that they were ignored for simplicity of analyses.

Independent variables

The category of household structure includes number of adult household members (16 years old or over) in a household, the proportion of male adults among the adults, household type (nuclear or extended), headship (female-headed or male-headed), headship by single parent, and presence of children and the elderly in a household. These factors are operationalized as follows.

- Number of adult household members, who were 16 or older at the time of interview

However, high school students are not included in the "adults" because the data does not include any information about their English or job training, which is necessary for major analyses in this research.

- Household type: extended or nuclear household.
- Headship: female headship or male headship.
- Presence of spouse of the head or not.
- Presence of children in the household whose age is under 16.

This variable is examined by three different age ranges of the children (less than 1, 1 to 5, and 6 to 15) in order to compare the relative importance of the three on the generation of multiple earners in the household.

- Presence of household members whose age is 65 and over or not.
- The percentage of males among the adult household members.

The category of human capital includes several kinds of human capital of household level such as age, education, English proficiency, length of English language training and job training, health condition, and length of residence in the United States. These variables are operationalized as follow.

- Average age of the adult household members.
- The percentage of adult(s) whose age is in the middle range, 25-45. This age range comes from the findings of prior research (Caplan et al., 1985; Majka and Mullan, 1992).
- The percentage of adult(s) whose poor physical or mental health condition has lasted for 6 or more months and limited the kind or amount of work at a job or prevented working at a job. This variable is based on questions Q.28a and Q.28b of the survey.
- Average years of schooling of the adult household members before coming to the United States. This variable is based on question Q.2a of the survey.
- Average weeks of English language instruction of the adult household members before coming to the U.S. This variable is based on question Q.4d of the survey.
- Average weeks of English language training taken in the U.S. by the adult household members. This variable is based on the question Q.4f of the survey.
- The percentage of adult household members whose English was relatively fluent at arrival among all adults in the household (Lower value is expected to be advantageous.) This variable is based on question Q.4a of the survey.

"At the time of arrival in the U.S., how well did you/she/he speak English?"

    "Very well" (1)
    "Well" (2)
    "Not well" (3)
    "Not at all" (4)

Fluency is defined here as "well" or "very well."

- The percentage of adult household members whose English was fluent at the time of interview among all adults in the household. This variable is based on question Q.4b of the survey. The criterion of the fluency is the same as the one for above variable.
- Average weeks of job training attended by the adult household members. This variable is based on question Q.24b of the survey.
- The number of months for the length of residence in the U.S. This variable is based on question Q.1j of the survey and the time the survey conducted (October, 1994). Therefore, the number of months for the length of residence in the U.S. can be calculated by the two kinds of information.

"What month and year did you/she/he enter the U.S. to stay?" (Q.1j)

The category of environment includes ethnicity of the household, first state of resettlement in the U.S., the availability to the household family of private or public transportation, and current participation in English language or job training and current enrollment in a school. The last factor, current enrollment, is predictable as a negative one to the generation of multiple earners although prior studies rarely mention it. These variables are operationalized as follow.

- Vietnamese households or non-Vietnamese households for the ethnicity of the households.

The ethnicity of the household is indicated by the country of birth of the household head. Therefore, this "ethnicity" is not a correct representation of ethnicity for all household members. However, this "ethnicity" is not necessarily a correct representation of ethnicity of all household members. However, by and large this measure does correctly represent ethnicity of household members. Especially, when the ethnic groups for analysis are divided into two (Vietnamese households and non-Vietnamese ones), the country of birth of household head is an almost perfect representation of the household members' ethnicity.

- The first state of resettlement is California (1) or not (0)

This variable is based on the following question from the survey:

"In what State did you (he or she) originally resettle?" (Q.1k)

This question was originally for refugee individuals. We could imagine that there may be different states for the first resettlement among household members. However, in the data, the household members in each household selected for the analyses are the same for the first state. Therefore, the first state for each household member means the one for the entire household.

Initially, this study was planned to examine the effect of residence of the refugee households on the generation of multiple earners. However, the states of current residence were not available from the data. In fact, because we may expect some extent of second migration (interstate movement after arrival from the state originally resettled), the information of the first state of resettlement may not represent perfectly the effect of residence (state) on the generation of multiple earners.

- The percentage of adult household members who have public or private transportation to get to work, job-training or school.

This variable is based on the following two questions in the survey.

"How many cars, vans or small trucks are kept at home that you (she or he) could use to get to work, job-training or school? (or that another household member could use to drive you/her/him to such activities) " (Q. 23a)

"Is there a bus stop, subway station, or other public transportation stop within a mile of this housing unit that you/she/he could use to get to work or other activities?" (Q.23b)

Unless somebody has no vehicle available for private use and no public transportation as described above, they are considered to have available transportation.

- The percentage of adult household members who are currently enrolled in English language or job training or in a school except a high school.

This variable is based on the following questions of the survey.

"Are (Is) you/she/he currently enrolled in an English language training program?" (Q.4j)   Yes or No

"Why are you/she/he not looking for a job? (multiple answer may be given) (Q.17)   Attending school or training

If a respondent indicated "Yes" for the Q.4j or "Attending school or training" as one of the reasons for not being in the labor force, this respondent is regarded as being enrolled.

VALIDITY AND RELIABILITY

As two important criteria for checking the quality of measurements, validity and reliability examine different aspects of the measurements. While validity concerns how the empirical measures adequately reflects the real meaning of the concept, reliability refers to the extent to which a measurement instrument yields the same results each time it is used (Babbie, 1990, pp. 132-135; Carmines and Zeller, 1979, pp. 11-13; Sanders and Pinhey, 1983, pp. 85-90).

According to the classification of the validity (Carmines and Zeller, 1979), the independent variables related to household structure can be said to have more "content validity" because they are generally considered as the ones indicating components of household structure. On the other hands, the independent variables of human capital or human capital investment can be said to have construct validity because they come from the theory of human capital. Environmental factors also have construct validity in that they have been examined and discussed in prior research with theoretical explanations. Although the factor of current enrollment has not been included in the prior studies, it can have a "face validity" as a constraint for the generation of multiple earner in the household because its negative effect can easily be predicted for the dependent variable.

Reliability seems to be very strong for the dependent and independent variables because these measurements can be understood relatively clearly compared to other kinds of measurements which measure attitudes or opinions of people. For example, such questions as "working last week or not last week," "What was your age at last birthday?," and "How many years of schooling did you complete before coming to the U.S.?" are not vague or confused. The actual measurements such as the number of adult household members, average age of the adult household members, and average years of schooling of the adult household members can also be reliable.

However, several things must be pointed out as factors which may lower the validity and reliability of the measurements.

First, English proficiency levels are measured not by certain kinds of objective techniques (e.g., kinds of test for spoken English) but by self-report. The questions for these are "At the time of arrival in the U.S. (or now), how well did (do/does) you/she/he speak English?" These questions, in general, cannot fail to contain some subjective opinions of the respondents, by which English language fluency of the self is generally compared to that of other refugees. In this perspective, the measurements may not be valid to measure English proficiency of the refugees.

Second, the information about all household members was collected through an interview with one adult household member. If the other household members were not on the same site, and if the actual interviewee did not have clear information about other household members, the responses from the person might not be reliable.

DATA TRANSFORMATION

Because this study analyzes primarily household-level information, the original data, which were collected for individual household members had to be transformed for household level. The following section describes the process for the data transformation.

Selection of households

In the creation of household variables, every household member's information must be given in the data set. For example, for the household with 5 members, if there is no information for one or several of them, this household cannot be used for the analyses based on a household. Therefore, to select households for whom every member was represented in the data was the first process in preparing for data transformations.

Two variables were used for household selection: household members' identification (ID) number and age. If ID numbers of household members were consecutive without any missing household members between the numbers (e.g., 3458.01, 3408.02, 3408.03, 3408.04), the household was kept for analyses. If there is (are) a missing household member(s) in a household (e.g., 3472.01, 3472.03, 3472.04, only three household members among four), the household was deleted from the analyses. Secondly, if there were missing responses (don't know or refuse to answer) for age information among household members, the households were deleted. This situation is possible because only one household member was contacted and information on every household member was acquired through that person. However, five households in which age information was missing for only one of the spouses were retained by replacing the missing responses for age by ages of another spouse in the same household. The major concern in the data selection and transformation was to retain as many households as possible in order to keep the data sizable to achieve more statistically significant analysis results and to keep the data similar to the original data set, which was weighted in terms of years of entry and ethnicity. Therefore, the 5 households, which were generally very usable for the analyses except for the age data, were retained.

Finally, among 677 Southeast Asian refugee households, 628 households were selected as appropriate cases for the study. These households contained 3255 household members, 64 percent of which were those who were 16 or older, except for high school students. This study excluded high school students (n=164) from the analyses because they were not appropriate to provide such information as experience and length of English language instruction and job training taken in the United States. We may guess that they had been or were being trained in terms of English language through an ESL (English as a Second Language) program and technical or vocational training within the high school. However, the information about these training experiences of high school students was not given in the data. Therefore, the high school students were excluded from the analyses although some of them had an experience of working since arrival or even were being employed at the time of interview.

Since original sample households were weighted according to year of entry and ethnic group, the case selection process for households may change the initial shape of distributions of the original sample households in the two kinds of characteristics. Fortunately, however, the distributions of years of entry and ethnicity for the selected households for this study were very similar to those of the original sample.[4] Therefore, the newly selected sample households can still be representative of the population of Southeast Asian refugee households which entered the United States from May, 1989 through April, 1994 in terms of years of entry and ethnicity. In general, weighted data by the year of entry and ethnicity were used for descriptive statistics primarily for presenting frequency distributions and mean values and unweighted data were used for inferential statistics, including group comparisons, correlations, and the logistic regression analyses.

Treatment of missing values

Since a major statistical analysis method for this study is logistic regression analyses, the households must have non-missing values for all independent variables for the logistic regression. Some of the independent variables for logistic regression equations were created on the basis of household members' individual information. For example, the average education year of potentially employable household members (who were 16 or older, except for high school students) was created by summing the years of education of all of those household members in a household and dividing the sum of education years by the number of those household members. In the process of data transformation, missing responses for a certain variable (e.g., years of schooling) of household members were replaced by the mean of the variable for the persons who were 16 or older but high school students (e.g., mean of the years of schooling for 2083 individuals).

DATA ANALYSIS

Descriptions of SEA refugee households

This section describes the characteristics of SEA refugee households and analyzes the household members' family status and labor status. This part of the analysis consists primarily of the frequency distribution analyses and comparisons such as t-test or Chi-square test results. Here the following information is included:

- The characteristics of household structure.
- Labor force status of household members by their family status.
- Distribution of the number of wage workers in the household.

- Composition of household wage labor in terms of family status.
- Presentation of the variation of welfare and poverty status of households by the change in the number of wage-earners in the household

Significant factors associated with the generation of multiple wage-earner generation

As mentioned earlier, the major research question of this study is why some Southeast Asian refugee households generate multiple earners while others fail to do so. Therefore, this part of the data analysis looks at what kinds of factors are influential in the generation of multiple wage-earners. In addition, this study looks for the factors which differentiate the SEA refugee households which cannot generate any wage-earner from those households which contain one wage-earner. Also, the factors will be sought which differentiate one wage-earner households from the households which can generate additional wage-earner(s).

The generation of multiple earners in the household is a kind of event occurring. Logistic regression estimates the probability of an event occurring by given independent variable(s) (SPSS, 1992). Through logistic regression, this study examines what factors (i.e., independent variables for this study) contribute positively or negatively to the generation of multiple earners in the household (i.e., one of dependent variables for this study) and examines to what extent the factors contribute to the event occurring. R statistic was used to examine the relative importance of each of the selected independent variables in predicting the dependent variable. R statistic means "the partial correlation between the dependent variable and each of the independent variables" (SPSS, 1992, p. 5) and ranges from -1 to +1 in value. The R statistic can be a pure contribution of the independent variable in a given regression model that other remaining independent variables are controlled. In other words, when other independent variables are constant, the contribution of the independent variable can be examined for its extent of independent contribution to the event occurring.

Logistic Regression Model

The logistic model of this study is written as below reflecting the basic form of the model.

logit $(Y) = B_0 + B_1X_1 + \ldots + B_kX_k$
(an expression of a basic logistic regression model)

logit (MULTIEMP) = $B_0 + (B_1)$NUMADULT + (B_2) MALEPERC + (B_3) EXTENDED + (B_4) MALEHEAD + (B_5) SINGLEMF + (B_6) PRES15-6 + (B_7) PRES5-1 + (B_8) PRESINFA + (B_9) PRESOLD + (B_{10}) MEANAGE + (B_{11}) PRIMEPER + (B_{12}) UNHEALTPER + (B_{13}) MEANEDUC + (B_{14}) ENGWEEHO + (B_{15}) ENGWEEUS + (B_{16}) ARRIVPER + (B_{17}) NOWPER + (B_{18}) JTWEEUS + (B_{19}) LENGTH + (B_{20}) FIRSTST + (B_{21}) ETHNIC + (B_{22}) ENROPER + (B_{23}) TRANSPER

In this model, the log odds of MULTIEMP (the major dependent variable, the presence of multiple earners in the household) is explained by the selected variables. B_0 is a constant of the equation and other B's from 1 to 23 indicate the logistic coefficients, which can be "interpreted as the change in the dependent variable, logit (Y), associated with a one-unit change in the independent variables" (Menard, 1995, p. 44).

The other two dependent variables (ONEEMP and ADDITIONAL; for detailed information and abbreviated names of every variables employed in this study, refer to table 3.1) are employed for the same logistic regression model. One of the independent variables, which was not described in the earlier section of this chapter, NUMADULT (number of adult household members) was selected in order to control the possible effect of that variable on the presence of multiple earners in the household.

The table below describes the dependent and independent variables for the logistic regression analyses.

For the independent variables with dichotomous values (for examples, EXTENDED, MALEHEAD, SINGLEMF, etc.), zero and one indicate a reference group and a comparison group, respectively (Hardy, 1993). Therefore, the regression coefficients of these dichotomous variables represent the characteristics of the comparison group.

The variables related to the percent (for example, MALEPER, PRIMEPER, UNHEALTPER, etc.) indicate the proportion of household members with certain characteristics among all household members who were 16 years old or older, but not high school students.

Table 3.1: Descriptions for independent variables

Variable Abbreviation	Description
NUMADULT	number of household members who were 16 or older except for high school students
MALEPERC	percent of male adult household members among the household members in the household
EXTENDED	extended households (1), in contrast to nuclear households (0)
MALEHEAD	male-headed households (1), in contrast to female-headed households (0)
SINGLEMF	households headed by single father or mother (1) or not (0)
PRES15-6	presence or absence of children aged from 15 to 6 yes (1) no (0)
PRES5-1	presence of children aged from 5 to 1, representing preschool children except for infant(s) yes (1) or no (0)
PRESINFA	presence of infant (s) in the household yes (1) or no (0)
PRESOLD	presence of the elderly in the household (65 years old or older) yes (1) or no (0)
MEANAGE	mean age of household members who were 16 or older (except for high school students) in the household
PRIMEPER	percent of prime aged (25-55) members in the household
UNHEALTPER	percent of physically or mentally unhealthy household members in the household
MEANEDUC	mean of the years of education for the household members who were 16 or older (except for high school students) in the household
ENGWEEHO	mean of weeks of English in the home country

Table 3.1 (continued)

Variable Abbreviation	Description
ENGWEEUS	mean of weeks of English in the United States
ARRIVPER	the proportion of household members who were fluent in English at the arrival time
NOWPER	the proportion of household members who were fluent in English at the interview time
JTWEEKUS	mean of weeks of job training in the United States
LENGTH	length of time in the United States (month)
ETHNIC	ethnicity of household members : Vietnamese (1) or nonVietnamese (0)
FIRSTST	the state in which a SEA household resettled initially California (1) or other states (0)
ENROLPER	percentage of enrolled members in a school (except for a high school) or an English or job training program
TRANSPER	percentage of household members who have available public or private transportation

Table 3.2: Descriptions for the dependent variables

Variable Abbreviation	Description
Dependent Variables	
MULTIEMP	presence of more than one wage earner in the household yes (1) or no (0)
ONEEMP	presence of no earner (0) or presence of only one earner (1)
ADDITIONAL	presence of one earner (0) or presence of two or more earners (1)

Therefore, for example, the variable PRIMEPER (the percent of household members whose age is 25 through 45) was formulated as follows:

PRIMEPER = (number of prime-aged household members / number of all household members who were 16 or older but not a high school student) * 100

Like PRIMEPER, other independent variables of percentage vary from 0 to 100 as a proportion of certain types of household members among all household members who were 16 or older except for high school students. The reason for selecting this type of independent variable is to avoid the effect of the number of the adult household members on the independent variables. If, rather than the percentages, the actual number of certain kinds of household members is used, the effect of the number of adults in the household cannot be avoided. It is expected that if there are 5 adult household members age 16 or older, the household is more likely to contain males than the households which have only two household adults. Therefore, the proportion of the males in the household is more reasonable than the actual number of males in terms of searching for significant factors in the generation of multiple earners in the household.

However, the independent variables related to percent or average are not perfectly free from the effect of the number of adult household members. For example, when a household has only 2 male adults, MALEPERC (the percent of male adults in the household) can be 100. However, for another household with two males among the three adults, MALEPERC is about 67 percent. Despite the same number of male adults (two for both households), the percentages of male adults are different (100 percent for the first case and 67 percent for the second case). That is, the number of the household members influences the values of those independent variables, in particular, the independent variables of percentage. In order to control for this effect, NUMADULT (the number of the adult household members) was included in the logistic equation model, and R statistic (a partial correlation of a certain independent variable with the dependent variable while all other remaining independent variables are constant) was examined for each of the selected independent variables. If the variable NUMADULT is included in the regression equation, this variable can be automatically controlled when the partial correlation of other independent variables is examined.

The number of adult household members must also be included in the logistic regression model because the number of earners in the household is significantly correlated with the NUMADULT (Pearson correlation coefficient, r = .49, p<.001). Therefore, the contribution of NUMADULT to the prediction for the dependent variable should also be examined in addition to those of other independent variables.

When the effect of NUMADULT on independent variables of percentage is expected to be automatically controlled by inserting the NUMADULT into the logistic regression equation, we may think it is possible to use the variables of actual numbers (e.g., the number of male adults in the household or the number of prime aged adults in the household) instead of the variables of percentage (e.g., MALEPERC, PRIMEPER, etc.). However, when the independent variables of actual number were used in the regression equation, a high level of multicollinearity was found among some of the variables. According to Menard (1995), collinearity is "a problem that arises when independent variables are correlated with one another"(p.65). Menard also mentions that "perfect collinearity means that at least one independent variable is a perfect linear combination of the others" (p. 65). If there is perfect collinearity in the regression model, regardless of whether a linear or a logistic regression model is used, "it is impossible to obtain a unique estimate of the regression coefficients" (Menard, 1995, p. 65). "Collinearity also tends to produce linear and logistic regression coefficients that appear to be unreasonably high" (Menard, 1995, p. 65). Tolerance statistic is an index indicating the level of Collinearity. Roughly, a tolerance of less than .20 is cause for concern; a tolerance of less than .10 generally indicates a serious collinearity problem.

From the results of the tolerance test (refer to notes in the end of this chpater)[5], variable set 1 created a very low level of tolerance statistic for NUMADULT (number of adult household members). This seems to be predictable because the variable NUMADULT is highly correlated with such other independent variables as NUMMALE (number of male adults in a household), NUMPRIME (number of adult household members whose age is in the prime-age range, 25-45), NUMENGHO (number of adult household members who had English language education in their home country), NUMENGUS (number of adult household members who has taken an English language instruction in the United States after arrival), etc. Therefore, it seems to be more desirable to select the variables of percentage instead of direct numbers. In conclusion, this study selected set 2 for the list of independent variables in logistic regression model.

In this study, in addition to all sample households, two different ethnic cohorts (Vietnamese vs. non-Vietnamese) of sample households were analyzed by the same logistic regression model as ad hoc analyses.

NOTES

1. This section is primarily based on the "Technical Note" describing the ORR survey and sampling procedures presented in the "Report to the Congress, FY 1994" (ORR, 1995, p. 67).

2. Strictly speaking, the ethnicity of Southeast Asian households is not a correct expression because the questions asked the household head's country of birth. However, when we divided the ethnic group into two, Vietnamese and non-Vietnamese Southeast Asian refugee households, the information of the country of birth of the head could reflect the ethnicity of the household almost correctly. Based on the Southeast Asian households selected for the dissertation, the households indicated as "Vietnamese household" contain 99.3 percent of household members who indicated their ethnicity is Vietnamese. The other 0.7 percent and 0.1 percent were Chinese and Cambodian, respectively. The households indicated as "non-Vietnamese household" do not contain any household members whose ethnicity is Vietnamese. Their specific ethnicity was Hmong (60.6%), Lao (30.2%), Cambodian (4.9%), Mien (2.6%), Chinese (0.6%), Burmese (0.5%), Karen (0.3%), or Thai (0.3%).

3. Because not all of the household members were listed in the data for some households, the actual number of all household members could be more than 3510. The households which did not contain the information for all of the household members were deleted from the analysis.

4. The following table compares the distributions of the original sample and the newly selected households for this study in terms of the year of entry and ethnic group. The presented proportions for both sample were weighted.

	Burma	Camb-odia	Hmong	Laos	Viet-nam	Total
1989		0.8 (0.7)	2.2 (2.3)	1.2 (1.1)	6.0 (6.5)	10.2 (10.5)
1990		0.3 (0.3)	1.8 (1.7)	2.2 (2.0)	17.9 (18.6)	22.2 (22.5)
1991			1.5 (1.6)	1.1 (1.2)	16.2 (15.6)	18.7 (18.3)
1992	0.1 (0.1)		3.0 (2.9)	0.2 (0.2)	17.4 (17.3)	20.7 (20.5)
1993			1.6 (1.7)	0.2 (0.2)	18.9 (19.2)	20.7 (21.1)
1994	0.2 (0.2)		1.0 (1.0)		6.2 (5.8)	7.4 (7.0)
Total	0.3 (0.3)	1.1 (1.0)	11.1 (11.2)	4.8 (4.6)	82.7 (82.9)	100.0 (100.0)

The proportions given in parentheses were the distributions of the original sample.

5. Comparison of tolerance statistic for two different sets of independent variables in the multiple linear regression analysis for a dependent variable (i.e., the number of household members who are employed).

Independent Variable Set 1		Independent Variable Set 2	
Independent Variables	Tolerance statistic	Independent Variables	Tolerance statistic
NUMADULT	.072215	NUMADULT	.572990
NUMMALE	.276234	MALEPERC	.794270
EXTENDED	.816752	EXTENDED	.797974
MALEHEAD	.720530	MALEHEAD	.692248
SINGLEMF	.734584	SINGLEMF	.718096
NUM15-6	.730782	PRES15-6	.701953
NUM5-1	.500941	PRES5-1	.484942
NUMINFANT	.780933	PRESINFA	.780764
NUMOLD	.695364	PRESOLD	.666351
MEANAGE	.609415	MEANAGE	.595614
NUMPRIME	.401866	PRIMEPER	.695513

Comparison of tolerance statistic for two different sets of independent
variables (continued)

UNHEALTH	.879677	UNHEALTPER	.914590
MEANEDUC	.497500	MEANEDUC	.486105
ENGWEEHO	.567774	ENGWEEHO	.558468
NUMENGHO	.454125	ENGHOPER	.523556
ENGWEEUS	.630405	ENGWEEUS	.549419
NUMENGUS	.378937	ENGUSPER	.557633
NUMARRIV	.766261	ARRIVPER	.821011
NUMNOW	.521432	NOWPERC	.711113
JTWEEKUS	.433004	JTWEEKUS	.378884
NUMJTUS	.442584	JTUSPERC	.395163
LENGTH	.725334	LENGTH	.700846
ETHNIC	.413164	ETHNIC	.378398
ENROLL	.535843	ENROLPER	.693804
TRANSPOR	.100336	TRANSPER	.692003
FIRSTST	.928049	FIRSTST	.925985

CHAPTER 4

Results of Data Analysis

This chapter consists largely of four parts of results from the data analyses: characteristics of Southeast Asian refugee (SEA) households, family and labor force status of SEA refugee household members, composition of multiple earners in the household, and predictors for multiple earner households generated from logistic regression analyses.

The first section introduces the characteristics of Southeast Asian refugee households in terms of household structure and composition, human capital of household level, and environmental factors related to their resettlement in the United States. The second part provides the information on the labor force status of household members, which is basic but fundamental to understanding the household wage labor organization. The third part analyzes and decomposes the composition of wage-earners in the Southeast Asian refugee household and searches for a prevailing composition for their multiple earners. The final section of this chapter primarily contains the results of logistic regressions to search significant factors in the generation of a multiple-earner household (abbreviated variable name: MULTIEMP). This part also includes the results of logistic regression for two other dependent variables: the generation of one wage-earner in the Southeast Asian refugee household (ONEEMP) and the generation of additional wage-earner(s) in the Southeast Asian refugee household (ADDITIONAL).

Table 4.1: Household structural characteristics of Southeast Asian refugee households and ethnic comparison[a]

	All households (n=803)	Vietnamese households (A) (82.7%)	Non-Vietnamese household (B) (17.3%)	significant difference between (A) & (B)
Household type				* (Chi-square test)
Nuclear family	83.7 %	84.3 %	80.9 %	
Extended family	10.5 %	9.3 %	16.8 %	
Single only	5.7 %	6.4 %	2.2 %	
Headship				
headed by male	79.2 %	77.1 %	89.3 %	* (Chi-square test)
headed by female	20.8 %	22.9 %	10.7 %	square test)
headed by one parent	7.8 %	7.8 %	7.9 %	ns (Chi-square test)
Household composition				
Average household size	5.1	4.8	6.6	*** (t-test)
Average number of adults	3.2	3.4	2.3	*** (t-test)
Average number of children				
15-6 years old	1.1	0.8	2.3	*** (t-test)
5-1 years old	0.5	0.2	1.6	*** (t-test)
Percent of households containing at least a child aged				
between 15-6	48.3 %	41.9 %	79.2 %	*** (Chi-square test)
between 5-1	26.2 %	17.5 %	68.7 %	*** (Chi-square test)
less than 1	9.4 %	5.0 %	30.4 %	*** (Chi-square test)
Percent of households containing the elderly	8.2 %	8.0 %	9.4 %	ns (Chi-square test)

Table 4.1 (continued)

	All house-holds (n=803)	Vietnamese households (A) (82.7%)	Non-Vietnamese household (B) (17.3%)	significant difference between A & B
First State[b]				ns (Chi-square test)
California	42.8 %	40.7 %	52.5 %	p=.050
Other states	57.2 %	59.3 %	47.5 %	

a. The frequencies and mean values presented in the table are based on the weighted data while the results of group comparisons (Chi-square tests or t-tests) used unweighted data.

b. 'First State' means the state in which a Southeast Asian household resettled initially.

* p $\leq$ .05   ** p $\leq$ .01   *** p $\leq$ .001

"ns" means not statistically significant for the difference in the mean values or in categorical distributions between Vietnamese and non-Vietnamese.

CHARACTERISTICS OF SOUTHEAST ASIAN REFUGEE HOUSEHOLDS

This section describes the characteristics of Southeast Asian refugee households in terms of household structure, human capital, and some environmental factors for Southeast Asian refugees. Some of prior studies have informed that there are considerable gaps between the Vietnamese and non-Vietnamese refugees in their socio-economic background and their achievements in the United States (ORR, 1994 and 1995; Potocky and McDonald, 1995). Therefore, this research also tried to compare these two groups of Southeast Asian households divided by ethnicity in the selected variables for this study.

Household type

The majority of Southeast Asian refugee households are nuclear family households (83.7 percent). Extended family households and households consisting of one single person comprise only 10.5 percent and 5.7 percent of all households, respectively. Vietnamese and non-Vietnamese SEA households are quite different. In particular, the proportions of extended family and single-alone households are significantly different for these types of households While the Vietnamese refugee group has a higher proportion of single-alone households than non-Vietnamese refugees, the former is considerably lower than the latter in the proportion of extended households. The distribution of household types of the Southeast Asian refugees in this study is very different from that of their predecessors. According to a prior study of Southeast Asian refugees (Caplan, Whitmore, and Bui, 1985), nuclear and extended family households were 48 percent and 27 percent of all sample households, respectively. Small proportions of the sample consisted of one-single households (4.7 percent) and the households of "unrelated singles" (5.5 percent). The composition of the remaining households (about 14 percent) was of a more complicated or heterogeneous composition—i.e. nuclear family plus single(s), extended family plus single(s), multiple families,

Table 4.2: SEA refugee household types for two different cohorts by the time of arrival.

	1978-1982 arrivals[a] (n=1,384)	1989-1994 arrivals [b] (n=803)
Single (one)	4.7	5.7
Unrelated singles	5.5	-
Nuclear family	48.2	83.7
Extended family	27.2	10.5
Multiple families	2.6	-
Nuclear family plus unrelated single(s)	5.1	-
Extended family plus unrelated single(s)	4.8	-
Multiple families plus unrelated single(s)	1.9	-
Total	100.0	100.0

a. Source: Caplan et al. (1985, p. 53).
b. The frequencies presented in the table are based on the weighted data.

and multiple families plus single(s).simple in the household types. There are no households which contain unrelated singles regardless of the type of household. Also, if the current study employs the definition of a nuclear family household defined by Caplan and his associates (1985), the proportion of nuclear households would increase because their definition included "possibly one grandparent," as a member of the nuclear family household, which the current study excluded. On the other hand, the proportion of extended family households in the current data is considerably smaller than the corresponding proportion in the prior data: 10.5 percent of the first vs. 27.2 percent for the latter.

Headship of Southeast Asian refugee households

Among all sample household heads, approximately eight out of ten are men. In terms of female headship, Vietnamese households (about 23 percent) are stronger than non-Vietnamese SEA households (about 11 percent). On the other hand, about eight percent of all households are headed by a single mother or single father and this trend is almost the same for both ethnic groups.

Household composition

The average household size of Southeast Asian refugee households is 5.1, which includes three adults and two children who are under 16 years old. Compared to family sizes of several ethnic or racial groups in the United States, the average household size of SEA refugee households is very large. For reference, according to the United States Census of 1990, family households of Whites contain on the average 3.06 persons, while Black families number 3.48. Even Asian and Pacific islander families in the United States consist of a smaller number of persons (3.80) than SEA refugee households.

In ethnic comparisons within the Southeast Asian refugee households, Vietnamese households contain more adults and fewer children than do non-Vietnamese SEA households: on the average, 3.4 adults and 1.1 children for the Vietnamese households ; 2.3 and 4.2 children for non-Vietnamese SEA households. More detailed divisions of children by age show that on the average Vietnamese households contain less than one child aged 15 through 6 years old or a preschool child while non-Vietnamese ones have 2.3 and 1.6 children for the corresponding age ranges.

Percentages of households which contain at least one child of each age range (from 15 to 6 years old, 5 to 1 year old, and less than 1 year old) are considerably higher for non-Vietnamese SEA households than Vietnamese ones. The differences in the household size (including average numbers of adults, children aged 15-6, preschool children, and infants and the percentage of households which have at least one child regardless of the age ranges) between the two ethnic groups were also very significant ($p \leq .000$).

The Southeast Asian refugee households in which elderly persons (65 or older) reside are about eight percent of all households. This proportion is similar for the two ethnic groups: 8.0 percent for Vietnamese and 9.4 percent for non-Vietnamese.

In summary, Southeast Asian refugee households contain a greater number of household members than other ethnic or racial groups in the United States. The size of non-Vietnamese SEA households was larger than Vietnamese ones, but this larger household size can be explained by the presence of significantly more children, regardless of the age ranges, and the presence of fewer adults than Vietnamese households. Non-Vietnamese SEA households are considerably higher than their counterpart in terms of the percent of households with at least one child. However, the two ethnic cohorts are not significantly different in the proportion of elderly members, which is about eight percent for all sample households.

When household composition is compared for different household types, the results are somewhat different. Extended households contain more household members (6.0) than nuclear ones (5.3) on the average. Also, extended households have more adults and children than nuclear households. However, these differences are statistically not significant according to the t-test. However, significant differences can be found in more specific components of the household composition such as in the number of preschool children, or in the percentages of households containing at least one preschool child, infant, or the elderly person. Particularly, the percent of households which contain at least one person who is 65 or older show the most significant difference between extended (29 percent) and nuclear households (5.5 percent) among the factors for household composition. In the comparison of Vietnamese households to non-Vietnamese ones, there was not significant difference in the percent of the households with at least one elderly person.

Table 4.3: Household composition by household type (nuclear and extended)[a]

	Nuclear households (A)	Extended households (B)	significance of difference between A& B
Average household size	5.3	6.0	ns (t-test)
Average number of adults	3.3	3.8	ns (t-test)
Average number of all children	1.7	1.8	ns (t-test)
Average number of children aged between 15-6	1.2	0.9	ns (t-test)
Average number of children aged between 5-1	0.5	0.7	* (t-test)
Percent of households containing at least a child aged			
between 15-6	52.8 %	38.6 %	ns (Chi-square)
between 5-1	27.4 %	32.6 %	* (Chi-square)
less than 1	9.3 %	14.8%	* (Chi-square)
Percent of households containing the elderly	5.5%	29.1%	*** (Chi-square)

a. The frequencies and mean values presented in the table are based on the weighted data while the results of group comparisons (Chi-square tests or t-tests) used unweighted data.

* $p \leq .05$.

** $p \leq .01$.

*** $p \leq .001$.

"ns" means not statistically significant.

In summary, there is no significant difference between nuclear and extended family households when the components of household composition are broadly compared, such as the household size and number of adults. However, the numbers of preschool children and of infants are factors which differentiate extended households from nuclear ones: the first contain slightly more preschool children in the household on the average than the latter and the first has a greater tendency to contain more preschool children or infants then the other. Extended households are also more apt to contain at least one of elderly person in the household. This difference is more significant than the difference in the number or presence of preschool children. However, the nuclear households also contain more than 5 persons on the average. This size of nuclear households is considerably bigger than the average size for each ethnic or racial American household mentioned early.

FAMILY STATUS OF HOUSEHOLD MEMBERS

Household heads

As noted before, the adult household members in this paper are those family members who are 16 years old or over, but are not high school students. Among these, a household head is defined as "the person who has overall responsibility, that is the person in whose name your home is rented, owned, or being bought" (refer to the Annual Survey provided in Appendix)[1]. The household heads in SEA refugee households are primarily adult household members who are married (85 percent) or have been married (7 percent). The remaining eight percent of all household heads are the adults who never married. Therefore, the household head is not necessarily a father or a mother or, if there are no children, a husband or a wife.

The proportion of never married household heads is higher for extended households and single-alone households than nuclear ones. The reason that extended households contain more never married household heads than nuclear ones do comes partly from the definition of extended households. By definition, extended households include households consisting of "related singles" (e.g., consisting only of siblings or relatives, without the presence of nuclear household members). If these households of related singles were excluded from the extended households cohort, the proportion of never married heads would be 8.2 percent.

Table 4.4: Marital status of household heads[a] unit: %

Marital status	All households	Nuclear households	Extended households	Single alone households
married	84.7	91.1	62.2	34.3
divorced, separated, and widowed	7.0	5.8	11.3	15.5
never married	8.2	3.0	26.5	49.0
other	.2	.1	.0	1.2
Total	100.0	100.0	100.0	100.0

a. The frequencies presented in the table are based on weighted data.

Adult household members other than the heads

The table 4.5 shows the relationship to the household head of the other household members who were 16 or over at the time of interview, but excluding high school students.

Nuclear households consist of household heads (30 percent) and their immediate family members (70 percent). More than 94 percent of the nonhead family members were spouses and children of household heads. More specifically, unmarried adult children comprise more than a half (56 percent) of all nonhead household members and the spouses of the heads account for 38 percent. The remaining about 6 percent of the nonhead household members are the parents or siblings of the head who is an adult child and never married.

For extended households, the composition of nuclear family members is similar to that of nuclear households. About 90 percent of the nuclear family members are the spouses (42.3 percent) or adult children (47.4 percent) of the heads. The parents or siblings of adult-child heads are about 10 percent of all nonhead nuclear family members. All of these nonhead nuclear family members comprise about 46 percent of all nonhead household members of extended family households. The remaining 54 percent of the nonhead family members are nonnuclear family members such as the parents or siblings (48 percent) of married household heads, the married children[2] and their spouses living with the heads (33 percent), and grandchildren or other relatives of the heads (19 percent).

Table 4.5: Relationship to the household head of nonhead household members.[a]

Value Label	Nuclear (N=1815)	Extended (N=234)	
Head of Household	30.4	26.2	
Other Family Members	69.6	73.8	
Nuclear family members	*100.0*	*46.2*	
parent(s) of the head	3.2		1.7
siblings	2.5		8.5
husband	4.4		3.9
wife	34.0		38.4
son	29.8		24.2
daughter	26.2		23.2
	100.0		100.0
Nonnuclear family members		*53.8*	
parent(s) or sibling(s) of married head			48.2
married children and their spouses			33.2
other relatives			18.6
			100.0
Total	100.0	100.0	100.0

a. The frequencies presented in the table are based on weighted data. (Unit : percent)

LABOR FORCE STATUS OF SOUTHEAST ASIAN REFUGEE HOUSEHOLD MEMBERS

Among all adult household members (16 years old or over, but not including high school students), about 38 percent of all household members are in labor force and the same proportion of all members

Table 4.6: Labor force status of SEA refugee household members[a]

	All adult household members (n=2567)	All household heads (n=798)
Percent of persons in labor force	38%	42 %
Percent of persons who had been employed since arrival	38%	41 %
Percent of persons being employed	34%	35 %
Average hours of work for all jobs per week	36.2 (n=767) min 5 max 72	36.3(n=270)
Percent of the employed who were working 40 or more hours per week	81 %	81 %
Average hourly wage for the prime job	$6.08 (n=666) min $3.50 max $19.00	$6.37 (n=242)
Average weekly wage income[b]	$219 (n=838) min $27.50 max $760.00	$229 (n=278)

a. The data on which the results were based were weighted by ethnicity and years of entry to the United States.

b. This variable was made by multiplying hours of work for all jobs per week by the hourly wage for the prime job. Missing cases (e.g. don't know or refuse to answer) were replaced by the average of all non-missing values.

Table 4.6 (continued)

	Heads of nuclear households (n=666)	Heads of extended households (n=86)	Heads of single alone households (n=46)
Percent of persons in labor force	40 %	40 %	65 %
Percent of persons who had been employed since arrival	39 %	44 %	62 %
Percent of persons being employed	33 %	35 %	65 %
Average hours of work for all jobs per week	35.7(n=209) min 5 max 60	38.4 (n=30) min 14 max 40	38.7 (n=30) min 20 max 66
Percent of the employed who were working 40 or more hours per week	79 %	94 %	86 %
Average hourly wage for the prime job	$6.32 (n=191) min $3.50 max 17.00	$6.60 (n= 28) min 4.25 max 17.0	$ 6.48(n=23) min $4.25 max $9.00
Average weekly wage income[b]	$224 (n=219) min $30.00 max $680.00	$255 (n=30) min $59.50 max $680.00	$245 (n=28) min $100.00 max $360.00

a. The data on which the results were based were weighted by ethnicity and years of entry to the United States.

b. This variable was made by multiplying hours of work for all jobs per week by the hourly wage for the prime job. Missing cases (e.g. don't know or refuse to answer) were replaced by the average of all non-missing values.

Table 4.6 (continued)

	All nonhead household members (n=1768)	Nonhead household members in nuclear households (n=1525)	Nonhead household members in extended households (n=243)
Percent of persons in labor force	37 %	39 %	26 %
Percent of persons who had been employed since arrival	37 %	39 %	27 %
Percent of persons being employed	33 %	34 %	24 %
Average hours of work for all jobs per week	36.1(n=497) min 5 max 72	36.0 (n=452) min 5 hours max 72 hours	36.8 (n=40) min 14 hours max 40 hours
Percent of the employed who were working 40 or more hours per week	81 %	81 %	85 %
Average hourly wage for the prime job	$ 5.92 (n=424) min $3.50 max $19.00	$5.90 (n=387) min $3.50 max $15.00	$6.09 (n= 38) min $4.25 max $19.00
Average weekly wage income[b]	$214 (n=561) min $27.50 max $760.00	$213 (n=507) min $27.50 max $600.00	$224 (n=53) min $84.00 max $760.00

a. The data on which the results were based were weighted by ethnicity and years of entry to the United States.

b. This variable was made by multiplying hours of work for all jobs per week by the hourly wage for the prime job. Missing cases (e.g. don't know or refuse to answer) were replaced by the average of all non-missing values.

have experienced working in the United States The proportion of the adult household members who were working is 34 percent.[3] They worked on the average 36.2 hours a week and they were paid $6.08 per hour. Consequently, they earn on the average $219 for their weekly wage income. Also, eight of ten workers were working 35 hours or more a week.

The rates of labor force participation, work experience since arrival, and employment for household heads seem to be slightly higher than for nonhead household members on the average. However, when Chi-square tests were conducted for the unweighted data, there were not significant differences between household heads and nonhead household members in terms of the three labor force status items. More considerable differences can be found when relatively high rates of the three labor force status items (65 percent, 62 percent, and 65 percent) for heads of single alone households are compared to those of other heads. Other large differences are the relatively low rates of the three types labor force status (26 percent, 27 percent, and 24 percent) for nonhead household members of extended households compared to those for the corresponding household members of nuclear households.

In order to find possible explanations for the difference between single alone household heads and other heads, several factors were examined. From the Oneway-ANOVA tests, the heads of single alone households are statistically younger than those of nuclear households and more likely to be from a Vietnamese household than those from extended households. In other variables related to human capital such as years of education year, English proficiency, the length of English language or job training, and physical and mental health conditions, the heads of single alone households are not significantly different from their counterparts in nuclear and extended households. On the basis of these findings, we may expect that a different household structure would be a plausible reason for the better status for the heads of single-alone households than the heads of the households which contain other family members. That is, compared to the heads of nuclear or extended households, their younger age should be a very positive factor in acquiring a better status in the labor market.

An interesting difference, as pointed above, is between two cohorts of nonhead household members (those in nuclear and extended households) in their three kinds of labor force status. Specifically, nonhead household members are apt to post lower figures for labor force participation, work experience since arrival, and current employment status when they are members of an extended household than when they are of a nuclear household. However, the differences are not consistent by the ethnicity of households. That is, the differences between nuclear and extended households for their nonhead members' labor force status are statistically significant only

Table 4.7: Household members' labor force status by ethnicity[a]

	Vietnamese household members				
	All members	Heads only	Nonhead members		
			total	nucl-ear	extend-ed
Percent of persons in labor force	41.2	41.8	40.9	42.4	27.3 (**)
Percent of persons who had been employed since arrival	41.5	41.8	41.3	42.7	29.0 (**)
Percent of persons being employed	37.9	37.9	39.9	39.1	26.2 (**)
	Non-Vietnamese household members				
	All members	Heads only	Nonhead members		
			total	nucl-ear	extend-ed
Percent of persons in labor force	19.5	23.6	16.4	18.5	11.4
Percent of persons who had been employed since arrival	16.6	18.9	14.8	15.4	13.5
Percent of persons being employed	10.0	10.9	9.3	9.6	8.6

a. The data was not weighted for t-tests.

(**) Statistically significant difference at p is less than .01.

for Vietnamese households which are contrasted to non-Vietnamese SEA households.

From table 4.7, three significant findings can be pointed out. The first one is that Vietnamese household members have significantly higher percentages than non-Vietnamese in the three kinds of labor force status for each of the three cohorts (i.e. for all household members, for household heads, and for nonhead household members). The second finding is that regardless of ethnicity there is no significant difference between household heads and nonhead household members in the three kinds of labor force status. Although the heads of non-Vietnamese SEA households show higher figures than nonhead household members in the three kinds of labor force status, these differences are not significant. The third one, most importantly, is that the lower labor force status of nonhead members of extended households compared to that of the corresponding cohort of nuclear households is clearer when they are Vietnamese household members than when they belong to other ethnic groups.

To search for factors which generate the difference between the nonhead members of nuclear households and those of extended households, t-tests were conducted for selected variables (refer to Table 4.8). These tests were limited to Vietnamese households because this ethnic cohort showed significant differences in labor force status between the two cohorts of household types. The t-test results indicate that the presence of dependent family members such as preschool children and the elderly and years of schooling are very important factors for differentiating the labor force status of nonhead members in nuclear households from those members in extended households, when the sample is limited to Vietnamese households. Specifically, the better labor force status of nonhead members in nuclear households can be most significantly explained by the more years of education in their home countries and fewer number of dependent family members such as preschool children or the elderly (indicating fewer family demands). The availability of transportation also proved to be important for the better labor force of Vietnamese nonhead members of nuclear households.

Other statistically significant factors are not simple to interpret. The research finding is that the first cohort, which shows better results in labor force, has a higher proportions of enrolled people in an English language or a job training or in a school except a high school than the latter cohort.

Table 4.8: Difference in the selected factors between nonhead household members of nuclear households and those of extended households (Vietnamese household members only)[a]

Variables	Nonhead household members in nuclear households	Nonhead household members in extended households
Household Composition		
Presence of children	42 %	50 %
Presence of preschool children	12 %	35 %***
Presence of the elderly	9 %	28 % ***
Human Capital		
Average age	32 years old	34 years old
Percent of prime aged (25-45) members in the household	39 %	43 %
Percent of physically or mentally unhealthy household members in the household	21 %	14 %*
Years of schooling in home countries	9.6 years	7.8 years ***
Mean of weeks of English language instruction in the home country	20 weeks	25 weeks
Mean of weeks of English language instruction in the US	25 weeks	25 weeks
English proficiency at arrival time	3.4	3.3
English proficiency now	2.6	2.6

a. Unweighted data were used for the t-tests. *p<.05, ** p<.01, *** p<.001 for the t statistic or Chi-square statistic.

Table 4.8 (continued)

Variables	Nonhead household members in nuclear households	Nonhead household members in extended households
Mean of weeks of job training in the US	1.9 weeks	1.1 weeks
Length of time in the US (month)	24 months	33 months***
Percentage of enrolled members in a school or an English or job training program	43 %	34 %*
Percentage of household members who have available public or private transportation	97%	91%*
Gender (women)	62%	62%
The state of initial resettlement (California)	40%	43%

a. Unweighted data were used for the t-tests. *p<.05, ** p<.01, ***
p<.001 for the t statistic or Chi-square statistic.

This finding may induce the belief that enrollment does not impact the labor force status, especially on employment. In fact, enrollment in an English language program was not a big barrier to employment for all adult household members. The labor force participation rates and employment rates of the household members who are currently enrolled in an English language program are almost the same as those of the household members who are not enrolled (38 percent vs. 39 percent for labor force participation; 33 percent vs. 34 percent for employment rate). However, because enrollment in other kinds of educational or job training programs is found to be a barrier to labor force participation and employment, the interpretation is not simple. The only possible explanation is that, among the nonhead members in nuclear households who are enrolled, a higher proportion are enrolled in an English language program, which does not influence labor force participation or employment, than the corresponding proportion for the nonhead members in extended households: 63.5 percent for the former and 52 percent for the latter. Due to the relatively higher proportion of current enrollees in an English language program among all kinds of enrollees, the nonhead members in nuclear households may maintain a better labor force status than their counterparts in extended households.

The nonhead members in nuclear households, whose labor force status is better than that of their counterparts in extended households, are found to have spent less time in the United States than their counterparts. Therefore, the prior research finding that those who spend more time in the United States are more likely to be better in labor force and economic status than recent arrivals, is not applicable to this sample.

The proportion of unhealthy people appears to be unreliable data because the proportion is higher for the nonhead members of nuclear households than those of extended households although the labor force status of the first cohort is better than the other.

In summary, in labor force status, household heads were not different from nonhead household members except for the fact that they were receiving higher hourly wages. When the household heads were classified by household type, those in single alone households were significantly higher compared to the heads in the other two types of households in labor force participation, employment, and work experience since arrival. However, nuclear and extended household heads were very similar in the three indices. For nonhead members in Vietnamese households, when they were divided by their household type and compared, nuclear household members were significantly superior to extended household members in labor force participation, employment, and work experience in the United States while the two cohorts were not significantly different in the number of work hours per week, hourly wage, and weekly wage income. Major influential factors for the significantly better status for nonhead family members in nuclear households were more years of schooling, less likelihood of living with preschool child(ren) or the elderly in a household, and, surprisingly, shorter time spent in the United States.

The labor force status has been described and compared for all, household heads, and nonhead household members by their ethnicity and household types to which they belonged. These descriptions have provided us with detailed information of the comparative labor force status for several cohorts of household members classified by their family status, household type, and their ethnicity and possible explanations for the differences have been found between or among the cohorts. Among the cohorts, nonhead household members have primarily been analyzed because their labor force status was significantly different by the household type (nuclear households vs. extended households). This difference was clearly found for Vietnamese refugees, who are the dominant group of Southeast Asian refugees in the sample population.

Here, we need to know more specific family status information (described as relation to the head, e.g., wife, husband, mother, father, son, etc.) about the nonhead household members who are participating in labor force or employed in order to know who among the nonhead family members could be a potential and actual earner in the households. In the table below, their labor force status is also reported separately when their household heads are employed and not employed.

From table 4.9, several interesting features can be pointed out. First, the labor force participation rates and employment rates of nonhead household members decrease by roughly on the average a half when the employment status of the head goes from being employed to being unemployed.

Second, the labor force participation and employment rates of nonnuclear family members (household members except the head, spouse of the head, and/or the children, and parent(s) or sibling(s) of a never married head.) are on the average never lower than those of nuclear family members except adult children of the head. The labor force status of nonnuclear members is more interesting when their labor force participation and employment status are examined in each case of employment status (i.e., employed or unemployed) of the head. When their heads are employed, they are very low in labor force status compared to the average labor force status of nuclear family members (i.e., 37.7 percent vs. 54.5 percent for labor force participation rates and 37.7 percent vs. 52.2 percent for employment rates). However, their labor force status is impressive compared to those of nuclear members when the heads are not employed. In the average labor force

Table 4.9: Proportion of the nonhead household members who are in labor force and are employed by the employment status of the head.[a]

Relation to head	All	Labor Force Participation Rate	
		when the head is employed	when the head is not employed
Nuclear family members	37.4%	54.5%	27.3%
husband (4%)	29.7	64.1%	19.4%
wife (32%)	28.2	54.7%	11.7%
children (51%)	44.7	56.4%	37.8%
other[b] (6%)	26.0	22.1%	20.4%
Nonnuclear family members (7%)	30.2	37.7%	25.4%
All (100%)	36.9	53.1%	27.1%

Relation to head	All	Employment-to-Population Ratio	
		when the head is employed	when the head is not employed
Nuclear family members	33.1%	52.2%	22.4%
husband (4%)	26.3	57.5%	15.9%
wife (32%)	22.9	50.8%	6.5%
children (51%)	41.1	55.2%	33.1%
other[b] (6%)	21.4	22.1%	17.8%
Nonnuclear family members (7%)	28.7	37.7%	23.0%
All (100%)	32.8	51.0%	22.5%

a. The percentages were calculated on the basis of weighted data.

b. OTHER indicates a father, a mother, and sibling(s) of the never married heads.

participation rate, they are very close to that of nuclear family members (i.e., 25.4 percent vs. 27.3 percent) and their employment rates are even slightly higher than those of their counterparts (i.e., 23.0 percent vs. 22.4 percent). Compared to the labor force participation rates and employment rates of specific family status (i.e., husband, wife, children, and other) of the nuclear family members, those of nonnuclear members are only behind the adult children in labor force participation and employment rates.

Third, among all nonnuclear family members, adult children (never married daughters or sons) are most likely to be in labor force or employed. Also, their relatively high rates of labor force participation and employment are generally maintained regardless of the employment status of the household head. In particular, when the household head is not employed, their labor force participation and employment rates are considerably higher than those of any other nonhead members.

Fourth, among the all kinds of cohorts classified by family status, the adult children and non-nuclear family members show relatively small amounts of decrease in their labor force participation and employment rates compared to the decrease for spouses of the heads.[4] That is, in the two different status of household heads' employment (i.e., employed or unemployed), the adult children and nonnuclear family members are more likely to be consistent than the spouses of the heads. This finding means that they are less likely be influenced by the employment status of the heads than other household members.

Fifth, when the household is headed by a wife, the labor force participation rate of the husband (29.7 percent) is not much higher than that (28.2 percent) of the wives whose husbands are the heads in the household. This means that whoever the head is (i.e., a husband or a wife), the labor force participation rates of the spouses are very similar and considerably lower than those of adult children.

DISTRIBUTION OF WAGE-EARNERS AMONG SEA REFUGEE HOUSEHOLDS

Until now this study have examined household members' labor force status by their family status such as household head, nonhead family members, nuclear family members or non nuclear family members, and even more specifically, spouses/adult children, and other family relationships to the household head. Also, we examined how the average rate of labor force status of those family members can be changed by the household head's employment status. These analyses provide information about the potential or actual earners among nonhead household members. However, since these analyses for individual household members are not enough to illuminate the labor organization of the household, we need to decompose the pooling of wage labor of the household while using the household as an analysis unit. First of all, the number of earners in a household will be examined to determine how extensively SEA refugee households try to generate multiple earners in a household.

About half the sample households are SEA refugee households which contain at least one wage-earner. Among the remaining households which contain two or more earners (28 percent of all sample households), 42 percent have only one earner and the other 58 percent two or more earners (i.e., multiple number of earners). These distributions of wage-earners for SEA refugee households are not much different from the corresponding distributions for nuclear households or extended households.

Table 4.10: Distribution of number of wage-earners among Southeast Asian refugee households.[a]

	All 100.0%	Nuclear 83.7%	Extended 10.5%	Vietnam 82.7%	Non-Vietnam 17.3%
No earner in the household	49 %	50 %	49%	42 %	82 %
One earner in the household	23 %	21 %	16%	25 %	14 %
Two or more earners in the household	28 %	29 %	35%	33 %	4 %
Total	100%	100%	100 %	100%	100%

a. The frequencies presented in the table are calculated using weighted data on the basis of years of entry and ethnicity of Southeast Asian households.

Also, the Chi-square test result shows that there is no significant difference in the wage-earner distributions between nuclear and extended households. In contrast, an ethnic difference for the distribution of wage-earners is statistically significant: while Vietnamese households are similar to the sample households in the wage-earner distribution, non-Vietnamese SEA households are primarily "no-earner" households and have a very small proportion of the households containing one earner or two or more earners. Roughly eight out of ten non-Vietnamese SEA households do not have any wage-earner in the household; the ethnic cohort contains only 4 percent of households with two wage-earners. Therefore, non-Vietnamese SEA households seem to struggle to generate just one earner in the household, not to mention getting one more household member in the labor market.

COMPOSITION OF MULTIPLE WAGE-EARNERS IN THE HOUSEHOLD.

The remaining tasks in analyzing the pooling of family wage labor in Southeast Asian refugee households are to decompose that wage labor pooling in terms of specific family status and to search for typical multiple wage-earner compositions among Southeast Asian refugee households.

Among the Southeast Asian refugee households which contain only one wage-earner, about 58 percent of the households have their sole source of wage income from the employment of the head. One out of four households with only one earner is supported by the wage income of an adult child. The family status of the sole wage-earner of the remaining households (16.5 percent) is the spouses of the household head. Only one household depends on a son-in-law as a wage-earner in the household.

Among two-earner households, a little more than a half have a wage labor composition of "husband and wife." Roughly one fifth of the wage-earners of the two-earner households are a parent and an adult child. Another one fifth of the two-earner households consists of only adult children for the dual wage-earners in the household. Therefore, about 40 percent of the dual-earner households include at least an adult child for the household wage income source. A relatively small proportion (9 percent) of the dual-earner households are supported by siblings of the heads. These sibling dependent households seem primarily to be households consisting of only singles who are related by family or kinship relations. When we consider the households which contain two or more wage-earners, the involvement of adult children in wage labor generation appears more distinguishable. While the proportion of the households whose wage-earner composition is "husband-wife only" decreases from 52 percent to 26 percent, the households including at least one adult child as one of the wage-earners goes up to about 70 %.

Table 4.11: Composition of wage-earners in SEA refugee households[a]

	Number of wage-earners in the household	Family composition of the earners
All sample households	one	head 58%, spouse of the head 16.5%, adult children 25.3 %, son-in-law 0.4 %
	two [a]	Husband + wife (52%) one parent + one adult child (19%) two children only (20%) siblings of the head (9%)
	two or more (multiple)[a]	husband + wife (26%) husband + wife + child(ren) (23%) one parent + child (ren) (21%) adult children only (25 %) siblings (5 %)
Nuclear households headed by married couple	one	one earner: parent 76%, child 24%
	two or more (multiple)	husband + wife (30%) husband + wife + child (ren) (26%) one parent + child (ren) (19%) adult children only (24 %)

a. Due to the difficulty in enumeration, unweighted data were used for the calculation of the percentages.

Some of the employed adult children are married or have been married and accordingly are classified as nonnuclear members who are expected to be a household head or a spouse of the head in another household rather than remain as the adult child of the head. Also some of the adult children in the households headed by a single parent are expected to be more likely asked to participate in labor force and get a job than those in two-parent family households. Therefore, in order to grasp more clearly the extent of labor force involvement of the adult children of Southeast Asian refugee households, only those adult children who belonged to nuclear households headed by a married couple were analyzed. However, the trend of vigorous participation of adult children continues for the nuclear households, which consist of two parents and/or never married adult child (ren). Among all multiple-earner (two or more earners) households, those nuclear households headed by two parents comprise about 84 percent. Among all nuclear households headed by two parents and containing two or more earners, only 30 percent include both the husband and the wife as the sole source of household wage income. However, the employment of adult children is again impressive among the nuclear households. About seven out of ten of the nuclear households contain a never married adult child or children for wage-earner(s).

Based on these features of wage labor composition among Southeast Asian refugee households, adult children, regardless of their marital status, seem to be very important as sole or co-earners in the household. This finding indicates that the husband-wife model of dual earners prevailing in American households is not applicable to the Southeast Asian refugee households, whose members are in the initial stage of resettlement in the United States Instead, it would be more appropriate to say that Southeast Asian refugee households in general greatly depend on adult children in generating the first earner (one fifth of all SEA refugee households generating one earner) and multiple earners (about 70 percent of all SEA refugee households generating multiple earners). In addition, one fifth of all SEA refugee households which generate multiple wage-earners depend only on adult children for household wage income.

THE MEANING OF MULTIPLE EARNERS FOR SEA
REFUGEE HOUSEHOLDS

This paper has concentrated on revealing the trend of labor force participation and employment status of Southeast Asian refugee household members and decomposing the household wage labor organization. Through these analyses, we have determined that the labor force status of family members and the composition of the multiple wage labor in the household can be different according to different household structures or ethnicity of households. Also, we have been able to find prevailing compositions of wage-earners among Southeast Asian refugee households in the early resettlement period.

The remaining part of this chapter answer the second research question: what are the significant factors which are associated with the generation of multiple earners in the SEA household? While most of the analyses conducted in the earlier part of this dissertation are for individuals defined by broad or specific family status (e.g., nuclear members, nonnuclear members, father, mother, children, etc.), logistic regressions in this section are based on the variables of a whole household.

One important subject to be discussed before presenting the results of the logistic regressions is the meaning of the criterion for the dependent variable: presence of at least two earners in the household (multiple-earner household) or absence of those in the household (no multiple-earner household).

In other words, due to the presence of multiple earners in the household, how can the economic conditions of the household be enhanced? To examine the economic status of Southeast Asian refugee households according to the presence or absence of multiple wage-earners, the following four indices were employed: 1) total working hours per week for the employed household members, 2) total weekly household income from all wage labor, 3) the proportion of households independent from public assistance programs, and 4) the proportion of households which are above the poverty line by wage income (in terms of a week). For the examination, the households which have only one adult household member were excluded because these households are constrained by the household structure in the generation of multiple earners.

Table 4.12: The meaning of presence of multiple wage-earners in the Southeast Asian refugee household[a]

	Number of wage-earner(s) in the household				
	no	one	two	3 or more	2 or more
	47.8%	21.0%	17.8%	13.4%	31.1%
Total working hours per week of the employed household members	-	32 hrs. (1.0)	72 hrs. (2.3)	156 hrs. (4.9)	108 hrs. (3.4)
Total weekly household income from all wage labor	-	$190 (1.0)	$455 (2.4)	$915 (4.8)	$653 (3.4)
Total household wage income divided by household size	-	$43 (1.0)	$115 (2.7)	$159 (3.7)	$134 (3.1)
The proportion of households independent from public assistance programs	6 % (.24)	25 % (1.0)	49 % (2.0)	57 % (2.3)	52 % (2.1)
The proportion of households which are above the poverty line by wage income (in terms of a week)	0.6 % (.05)	12 % (1.0)	75 % (6.3)	96 % (8.0)	84 % (7.0)

a. The results presented in the table are calculated using weighted data on the basis of years of entry and ethnicity of Southeast Asian refugee households

The total weekly working hours of earners in the household are presented to examine the quality of work: a proportional increase of total work hours by the increase of the number of workers in the household. As shown in the table, when there are two and three or more earners in the household, the total work hours are on the average 2.3 times and nearly 5 times more, respectively, than that of a one-earner household. Total work hours for all multiple-earner (two or more earners) households is 3.4 times more than that of the one-earner households on the average. Therefore, the increase of wage-earners in the household means a proportional or more than proportional increase in total work hours. That is, the number of wage-earners seems to reflect the quality of employment.

The increase of total household income from wage incomes is similar to the increase of total work hours by wage-earners in the household. When only one wage-earner exists in the household, total wage income for the household is $190 per week. However, when there are two and more than two wage-earners in the household, the total wage income increases by more than a proportional trend: 2.3 times and 4.8 times that of the first households on the average, respectively. For all multiple-wage-earner households, the average of the total household wage income is 3.4 times more than that of single-earner households.

The total household wage income divided by household size can be more meaningful than the total household wage-income itself because the first kind of income reflects the amount of money which can be spent by each household member.[5] When the total household wage income is divided by the number of al household members including children, multiple-earner households are still better off than nonmnultiple wage-earner households while keeping the trend of the increase with more than proportional trend. For example, the average amount of money which each household member in multiple wage-earner households can use per week is $134. This amount of income is about three times more than that of one-earner household members on the average.

The proportion of households on public assistance and above the poverty line are also very good indices for representing the economic advantage of the multiple wage-earner household among Southeast Asian refugee households. SEA refugee households which contain two (49 percent) and more than two wage-earners more (57 percent), respectively, can be independent from public assistance according to the statistics. These proportions are significantly higher than those of no-earner (6 percent) or one-earner households (25 percent).

Finally, when the total weekly household wage incomes are compared to the official poverty guidelines, the meaning of the presence of multiple-earners in the Southeast Asian refugee households becomes clearer. Although only 12 percent of households with one wage-earner are above the poverty guidelines, when there exist two or more earners in the household, more than 80 percent of the households can exit the poverty thresholds.

In summary, the fact that there are two or more wage-earners in the Southeast Asian refugee household is very significant in terms of several indices of the economic status of the household. Particularly, when there exist two or more earners in the household, the extent of welfare independence is more than 50 percent, which is double that for one wage-earner households. Also, when weekly household wage incomes are compared to the poverty guidelines adjusted for the weekly amount, seven times more SEA refugee households are above poverty lines when there are multiple wage-earners in the household than when only one earner exists.

SIGNIFICANT FACTORS ASSOCIATED WITH THE GENERATION OF MULTIPLE WAGE-EARNERS

The table presented below include three kinds of dependent variables: MULTIEMP (generation of two or more wage-earners), ONEEMP (generation of one wage-earner), and ADDITIONAL (generation of additional wage-earner(s)). The reason for adding the two more dependent variables, ONEEMP and ADDITIONAL, in this study is to show possibly different lists of important predictors according to different goals of wage-earner generation, which can be overlooked in the logistic regression analysis for the dependent variable MULTIEMP.

The log of the odds of an event occurring is called a logit and the logistic regression model can be written by the logit as follows (SPSS, 1992, p. 6):

$$\log\left(\frac{\text{prob (event)}}{\text{prob (no event)}}\right) = B_0 + B_1 X_1 + \ldots + B_P X_P$$

For example, the log odds of "generating two or more wage-earners in the SEA refugee household (MULTIEMP)" can be written as follows:

logit (MULTIEMP) = -1.6002 + (.3707) NUMADULT + (.0109) MALEPERC + . . . + (-.0177) ENROLPER + (-.6388) TRANSPER

Table 4.13: Results of logistic regression analyses for the three different dependent variables[a]

Variable	MULTIEMP No or one earner (0) vs. two or more earners (1)		
	B	Exp(B)	R
Household Structure			
NUMADULT	.3707	1.4488	.1509***
MALEPERC	.0109	1.0110	.0203
EXTENDED	.1944	1.2146	.0000
MALEHEAD	.0111	1.0111	.0000
SINGLEMF	-.1098	.8960	.0000
PRES15-6	-.5661	.5677	-.0714*
PRES5-1	-1.2866	.2762	-.1185***
PRESINFA	-.4254	.6535	.0000
PRESOLD	-.9036	.4051	-.0422+
Human Capital			
MEANAGE	-.0224	.9779	.0000
PRIMEPER	.0075	1.0076	.0497+
UNHEALTPER	-.0054	.9946	-.0311
MEANEDUC	.0968	1.1016	.0627*
ENGWEEHO	.0068	1.0069	.0437+
ENGWEEUS	.0079	1.0079	.0435+
ARRIVPER	-.0085	.9915	.0000
NOWPER	.0118	1.0118	.1246***
JTWEEKUS	-.0132	.9869	.0000
LENGTH	-.0129	.9872	-.0349+
Environmental			
FIRSTST(CA)	-.8928	.4095	-.1299***
ETHNIC(VM)	.6392	1.8951	.0000
ENROLPER	-.0177	.9824	-.1663***
TRANSPER	-.6388	.5279	.0000
Constant	-1.6002		
-2 Log Likelihood	490.355		
Chi-Square	213. 74		
Number of observation	552		

a. The logistic regression results are based on the unweighted data.

$+ p \le .10$, $* p \le .05$, $** p \le .01$, and $*** p \le .001$.

Table 4.13 (continued)

Variable	ONEEMP No earner (0) vs. one earner (1)		ADDITIONAL One earner (0) vs. two or more earners (1)	
	Exp(B)	R	Exp(B)	R
Household Structure				
NUMADULT	.9091	.0000	1.6854	.1912***
MALEPERC	1.0053	.0000	1.0092	.0000
EXTENDED	1.3076	.0000	1.6458	.0000
MALEHEAD	1.3529	.0000	.8676	.0000
SINGLEMF	.6057	.0000	1.1398	.0000
PRES15-6	.6734	.0000	.7352	.0000
PRES5-1	.7684	.0000	.2543	-.1312**
PRESINFA	1.0329	.0000	.6585	.0000
PRESOLD	1.4242	.0000	.3264	-.0510+
Human Capital				
MEANAGE	.9677	-.0408+	.9836	.0000
PRIMEPER	1.0037	.0000	1.0098	.0609+
UNHEALTPER	.9990	.0000	.9931	-.0405
MEANEDUC	1.0616	.0000	1.0907	.0318
ENGWEEHO	.9957	.0000	1.0072	.0231
ENGWEEUS	1.0045	.0000	1.0057	.0000
ARRIVPER	1.0084	.0000	.9916	.0000
NOWPER	1.0077	.0577+	1.0093	.0856*
JTWEEKUS	1.0166	.0000	.9811	.0000
LENGTH	1.0037	.0000	.9879	.0000
Environmental				
FIRSTST(CA)	.4989	-.1065**	.4715	-.0922*
ETHNIC(VM)	2.4595	.0485*	1.3542	.0000
ENROLPER	.9806	-.2060***	.9919	-.0317
TRANSPER	1.0787	.0000	.4141	.0000
Constant				
-2 Log Likelihood	379.88		296.45	
Chi-Square	68.33		93.23	
Number of observation	367		295	

a. The logistic regression results are based on the unweighted data.

$+ p \leq .10, * p \leq .05, ** p \leq .01,$ and $*** p \leq .001.$

MULTIEMP: absence (0) or presence (1) of two or more wage-earners in the household

ONEEMP: generation of no wage-earner (0) or one wage-earner (1) in the household

ADDITIONAL: generation of one wage-earner (0) or two or more wage-earner (1) in the household

This model is statistically significant in predicting the selected dependent variable, MULTIEMP (generation of at least two wage-earners in the household), because the model Chi-square (x^2 = 213.735, df = 23) is statistically significant (p = .0000). Therefore, we reject the null hypothesis that the independent variables taken together have no relationship to the dependent variable. Also, this modeling can classify about 88 percent of nonmultiple wage-earner households (households which generates no or only one wage-earner) and about 61 percent of multiple wage-earner households correctly. Overall, about 79 percent of all sample households are classified correctly by the model of logistic regression.

In the logistic regression a logistic coefficient (B) means, like the linear regression coefficient, the change in the dependent variable (i.e., the change in the log odds of an event occurring) associated with a one-unit change in the independent variable (Menard, 1995, p. 43; SPSS, 1992, p. 6). Therefore, for example, a one-unit increase in NUMADULT is associated with an increase of .3707 in logit (MULTIEMP). This means that when the unit number of adults in a household increases from zero to one and the values of the other independent variables remain the same, the log odds of a SEA refugee household to generate two or more workers increase by 0.3707.

The statistical significance of the logistic coefficients comes from the significance of *Wald* statistics, although table 4.12 did not offer the statistics. *Wald* is a criterion on which the test that a coefficient for each independent variable is 0 is based. Therefore, if the *Wald* statistic is significant in a significance level (e.g., p ≤ .10 or.05 or .001), a hypothesis that the coefficient is 0 can be rejected, and the corresponding independent variable can be considered as a significant factor for predicting the given dependent variable (SPSS, 1992, p. 5).

As a similar statistic to the logistic coefficients (B), Exp (B) is used, indicating an odds ratio (Menard, 1995, p. 49). An odds ratio greater than 1 indicates that the odds of being a household of generating multiple earners increase when the independent variable increases. If the odds ration is less than 1, the reverse case will be true. When the factor equals 1, the odds will not be unchanged (SPSS. 1992, p. 7). For example, when a SEA refugee household is an extended one, the odds of being a multiple- earner household increase by 21.5 percent, although it is not significant statistically. For another example, the presence of at least one child whose age is between 15 and 6 results in a 43.2 percent decrease in the odds of being a multiple-earner household. This result is statistically significant.

However, neither the logistic coefficients nor the odds ratios can be used to compare the relative importance of each independent variable in the prediction of the dependent variable because the coefficients are based on independent variables whose units are not the same. The odds ratios have the same problem because they are providing "the same ordering, from the strongest to weakest, as the unstandardized logistic regression coefficient, once all of the odds ratios are transformed to be greater than 1 (or all less than 1)" (Menard, 1995, p. 49).

As one of the statistics produced by the logistic regression analysis, R statistic, which is analogous to "Beta" (a standardized coefficient in the linear regression), is appropriate to be used for the comparison of relative importance of given independent variables for the prediction of an event occurring. R ranges -1 to +1 in value. A positive value for the R represents that "as the variable increases in value, so does the likelihood of the event occurring" (SPSS, 1992, p. 5). When R value is negative, the opposite is true. "Small values for R indicate that the variable has a small partial contribution to the model" (SPSS, 1992, p. 5).

Based on the meaning of these statistics, we can find several independent variables with a statistically significant logistic coefficient and compare their relative contributions to predict the dependent variables. The significance level used in the analysis was 0.10 or less for the alpha value.

The independent variables which are associated with the dependent variable MULTIEMP (the generation of multiple wage-earners in the SEA refugee household) are ENROLPER, NUMADULT, FIRSTST, NOWPER, PRES5-1, PRES15-6, MEANEDUC, PRIMEPER, ENGWEEHO, ENGWEEUS, PRESOLD, and LENGTH when the statistical significance level is 0.10 or less. When we are more strict in the statistical tests, that is, we accept only a significance level of .05 or less, only the variables bolded are significant in predicting the dependent variable. NUMADULT and ENROLPER are two most influential variables. More adult household members and a higher percentage of the adult household members currently enrolled in a school (except a high school) or language or vocational training increases and decreases the odds of generating multiple earners in the household, respectively. In fact, these variables were entered in the regression model to control sample households in terms of these two factors rather than to examine their relative importance in the prediction. However, unexpectedly, NUMADULT was not related to the generation of one wage-earner (ONEEMP) but a very important predictor for the generation of additional earners (ADDITIONAL). When this study additionally examined the relative importance of this variable NUMADULT for the transition from a one wage-earner household to two wage-earner households, the variable was not significant. These findings mean that the factor of the number of adult household members cannot be a significant factor for the transition from no-earner to one-earner and from one-earner to two-earners as the generation of wage-earners in the SEA refugee households.

Except for the two variables, the first state of initial resettlement (FIRSTST) as a proxy factor for the current residence is the most important factor for the generation of multiple wage-earners for Southeast Asian refugee households. If a household resettled first in California, the odds of being a multiple-earner household decrease about 59 percent (Exp (B) = .41) compared to initial resettlement in the other states. With a similar magnitude of relative importance, the variable NOWPER (the percent of adult household members who currently have English proficiency) was found as a significant factor of the dependent variable. When the proportion of the fluent household members increases ten percent, the odds also increase approximately 12 percent because Exp(B) (=1.0118, about 1.012) indicates a 1.2 percent increase in the odds by a one percent change in the independent variable.

A similarly important variable among the independent variables of household structure is the presence of a preschool child(ren) in the household. If there is at least one preschool child in the household, the odds of being a multiple-earner household decrease by 72 percent compared to no-preschool-child households.

The presence of comparatively older children (aged 15 through 6) in the household and household average of schooling years before coming to the United States are similar in relative importance as predictors for the generation of multiple earners. R statistic for the first variable is -.0714 and for the other is .0627. These two variables are less important than the presence of preschool child(ren) in the domain of household structure and than the proportion of currently English proficient household members in the domain of human capital on the household level, respectively.

If we accept only a significance value of .05 (= p), statistically important factors are the presence of children in the household (PRES5-1 and PRES15-6) as household structural variables, current English proficiency (NOWPER) and education in the home countries (MEANEDUC) as household-level human capital, and the initial resettlement state (FIRSTST), except for two variables NUMADULT and ENROLPER.

If we can expand the level of statistical significance to .10 (= p), one more household structural variable and four more human capital variables can be included in the list of important variables for the prediction of the dependent variable, although their relative importance levels are lower than those accepted by a stricter criterion of statistical significance (p < .05). The presence of the elderly in the household (PRESOLD) can pose a barrier to generate two wage-earners with less statistical significance. With similar magnitude of relative importance, such human capital variables as the proportion of prime aged household members (PRIMEPER), household average number of weeks for English education taken before (ENGWEEHO) and after coming to the United States (ENGWEEUS), have a positive impact on the generation of multiple-earner households. Holding the least value of relative importance, the length of time in the United States since arrival (LENGTH) has a negative influence on the generation of multiple earners in the SEA refugee household. That is, more recently arrived refugee households have advantages in terms of generating two or more wage-earners than their predecessors within about 5 years of arrival in the United States.

Significant factors associated with the generation of one wage-earner in the households (ONEEMP) few compared to those found in the logistic regression for MULTIEMP. The most significant factors come from the domain of environmental factors: ENROLPER (R= -.2060), FIRSTST (California, R= -.1065), and ETHNIC (Vietnamese,

R=.0485). These variables are the only factors which are significant at the significance level (p) of .05 or less. As in the list of relatively important factors for MULTIEMP, the independent variables ENROLPER and FIRSTST (California) are still very significant to decrease and increase, respectively, the odds of being a one-earner household. However, unlike the results from the logistic regression for MULTIEMP, the ethnicity of the household (i.e., Vietnamese) is found to be a significant predictor for the generation of one wage-earner. These results mean that to be a Vietnamese household is still a facilitator for the transition from no to one wage-earner in the household even when household structure, human capital of household level, and the remaining selected independent variables in the domain of refugee environments are considered. In contrast, none of the selected variables in the domain of household structure were influential in the transition from no-earner households to one-earner ones.

Among the independent variables of human capital on the household level, with less magnitude of relative importance (also, only significant at p is .10 or less), the average age of adult household members (MEANAGE) and the proportion of household members who are fluent in English at the time of interview (NOWPER) are statistically significant. In other words, the younger the average age of adult household members and the greater the proportion of those in the household who are currently fluent in English, the more likelihood the household transits from a no earner to a one-earner household.

As significant factors which are associated with the generation of additional wage-earners (ADDITIONAL), if the variable NUMADULT is set aside, the presence of preschool aged children (R = -.1312) and the elderly (R = -.0510) in the household and initial resettlement in California (R = -.0922) are important, which negatively influence the generation of additional earners. Also, the proportion of currently English-fluent household members (NOWPER, R = .0856) and the proportion of those who are in the prime age range (25-45) are found to be statistically significant predictors, which increase the odds of generating additional wage-earner(s) in the household.

Comparing the relatively important predictors for the last two different dependent variables, transition from no to one-earner households (ONEEMP), and the transition from one to two wage-earners households (ADDITIONAL), we can find several interesting points.

First, the variables in the domain of environments (such as FIRSTST, ETHNIC and ENROLPER) are very critical factors for the generation of one wage-earner in the SEA refugee households while these variables are not or less important for producing additional wage-earners in the household. Second, while household structure appears not important for the generation of the first wage-earner, the presence of preschool aged children (PRES5-1) is found to be a very important barrier for transiting from one-earner households to multiple-earner households. Third, as one of the variables of human capital on the household level, the proportion of household members who are currently fluent in English (NOWPER) is important for both dependent variables ONEEMP and ADDITIONAL. However, this variable is more significant in generating an additional earner in the household (p< .05) than in producing the first earner in the household (p < .10). This means that current English language fluency becomes a more sensitive factor for the generation of multiple wage-earners in a SEA refugee household than for creating the first earner in the household.

Based on the model Chi-square values, the logistic regression model initially given for MULTIEMP is also statistically significant for both additional dependent variables, ONEEMP and ADDITIONAL (Chi-square values of 68.323 and 37.569, respectively, and p < .05 for both).

Additionally, this study attempted to conduct logistic regressions with the same model for the two different two ethnic groups (i.e., Vietnamese and non-Vietnamese SEA households). However, the sample size of non-Vietnamese SEA refugee households is too small in the sample size to attain the results from the regression analyses. Therefore, instead of examining every independent variable initially selected in the regression, the three domains of the independent variables were analyzed separately and the dependent variable was also limited to only ONEEMP (the generation of one wage-earner in the household). The three models for predicting ONEEMP are: Model 1, which consists of the variables of household structure only; Model 2, which consists of the variables of household-level human capital; and Model 3, which includes only the variables of refugee environments. Although the separated three logistic regression models

Table 4.14: Significant factors associated with the generation of one wage-earners in the non-Vietnamese refugee households[a]

	ONEEMP		
	No earner households (0) vs. one-earner households (1)		
	MODEL 1	MODEL 2	MODEL 3
	R	R	R
Household Structure			
NUMADULT	.0000		
MALEPERC	.2360*		
EXTENDED	.0000		
MALEHEAD	.0000		
SINGLEMF	.0000		
PRES15-6	.0000		
PRES5-1	.0355		
PRESINFA	.0000		
PRESOLD	.1263+		
Human capital			
NUMADULT		.2286*	
MEANAGE		.0000	
PRIMEPER		.0000	
UNHEALTPER		.0000	
MEANEDUC		.0000	
ENGWEEHO		.0000	
ENGWEEUS		.0000	
ARRIVPER		.0000	
NOWPER		.0000	
JTWEEKUS		.0000	
LENGTH		.2678**	
Environmental			
NUMADULT			.2492*
FIRSTST(CA)			-.2004*
ENROLPER			-.2436*
TRANSPER			.0000
-2 LL	48.800	46.955	46.270
Model Chi-Square	16.417+	18.262+	18.946***
N of observation	84	84	84

a. The logistic regression results are based on the unweighted data.
+ p $\leq$ .10, * p $\leq$ .05, ** p $\leq$ .01, and *** p $\leq$ .001.

cannot compare all initially given independent variables, within each of the three domains we can find which ones are more important for predicting a one-earner household.

Vietnamese households are so close to all the households in the sample size that the logistic regression results are generally similar to the whole sample in the list of relatively important predictors for the dependent variables, MULTIEMP, ONEEMP, and ADDITIONAL. Therefore, the results of the logistic regression analyses are not presented here. Only are the results for non-Vietnamese refugee households are provided in this section.

Statistically significant variables among the variables of Model 1 (household structure) are the proportion of adult men among all adult household members (MALEPER) and the presence of the elderly (PRESOLD). The first variable is more significant (p < .05) than the other (p < .10). Unexpectedly, when there is/are (a) household member(s) who are 65 or over, the household has more probability of generating one wage-earner than the households which do not contain the elderly. However, this factor cannot be significant if the significance criterion becomes stricter than .10 or less (i.e. p is equal to or less than .05).

In Model 2 (household-level human capital), except for NUMADULT, the length of time in the United States since arrival is found to be very significant in generating one wage-earner in the non-Vietnamese refugee households. Unlike the whole sample households, the non-Vietnamese ones are found to be in a better economic position if they have relatively long resided in the United States since arrival.

FIRSTST (California) and ENROLPER in the Model 3 are also significant for the generation of one wage-earner in the non-Vietnamese refugee households, if NUMADULT, which is included in the model in order to control the effect of the number of adult household members in the dependent variable, is set aside.

Overall, Model 3 (environmental factors) is better than Model 1 or Model 2 in terms of the prediction of the given dependent variable. In terms of the significance of model Chi-square and of classification correctness by the model, Model 3 provides better features: the first two models are less significant (p < .10) for the model Chi-square and lower for the classification correctness (90 and 88 percent, respectively, compared to 93 percent). In this context, the model consisted of the variables of environments (i.e., FIRSTST and ENROLPER) and fits better the dependent variable than the other two models, which indicate that other two remaining domains (i.e., household structure and human capital of household level), in non-Vietnamese SEA households can be said to be similar to Vietnamese ones. However, non-Vietnamese SEA households are found to be significantly influenced by such factors as MALEPER or LENGTH. This is the difference between the whole sample households and non-Vietnamese ones in the list of predictors for the generation of one wage-earner.

NOTES

1. Two households indicate non-adult daughters (ages 13 and 15 respectively) as their household heads. In these two cases, the heads designated originally were discarded and replaced by the father or the mother (if there is no father) because this study selects only persons who were 16 or over as possible labor force members. Also, another two households designated both spouses (husband and wife) as co-household heads.

2. Married children living with their parent(s) were considered extended family members even if they did not live with their spouses or children.

3. Among 2083 household members who were 16 or older, 578 persons responded the sorts of jobs (e.g. private company, government employee, self-employed, etc.). Among the 578 persons, 83.4 percent were or had been employed by private companies, and 15.4 percent were employed by governments. Only 0.7 percent were self-employed. In addition, there were no persons who had been working or had worked the last 12 months without pay in a family business. Therefore, most of the persons who reported that they were working at the time of interview seemed to be wage-earners.

4. Although "OTHERS" also, show relatively very consistent labor force status regardless of the employment status of the head, they are actually one of the specifically designated family members in the nuclear households (i.e., husband, wife, or children) because their family status is defined differently only due to the characteristics of the heads (i.e., never married adult children). Therefore, here, this cohort is temporarily excluded for the comparison.

5. Strictly speaking, this does not mean disposable income since the gross weekly wage calculated in this study is before taxes.

CHAPTER 5

Discussion and Conclusion

SUMMARY OF FINDINGS

Analyses of wage labor organization among SEA refugee households

First, the sample households analyzed for this study are more straightforward in their household composition when compared to findings of prior studies. There are no households composed of unrelated single(s) or multiple families (i.e., two unrelated families). Also, compared to the prior sample (Caplan et al, 1985; Caplan et al, 1990), extended households comprise a relatively small proportion among all sample households: about 27 percent for the prior sample and 11 percent for the current one. Consequently, the proportion of nuclear households is considerably larger compared to the prior sample: 84 percent vs. 48 percent. In the ethnic comparison, non-Vietnamese households are significantly more likely to be extended households than Vietnamese households.

Second, non-Vietnamese SEA households contain, on the average more children and fewer adults than Vietnamese households, more specifically, about four children vs. one child and 2.3 vs. 3.4 adults who are 16 or over but excluding high school students. More detailed comparison of household composition reveals that non-Vietnamese SEA households have more older children (aged 6 to 15) and preschool children (aged 1 to 5) than Vietnamese ones, and the proportion of the households containing at least one child and infant. The proportion of households containing elderly is, however, similar for Vietnamese and non-Vietnamese SEA households.

Analysis of human capital at the household level and environmental variables indicate non-Vietnamese SEA households are significantly more disadvantaged than Vietnamese households in the average years of education, the proportion of household members who are currently fluent in English, health condition, the proportion of prime-aged (24-45) household members, and the availability of transportation. Non-Vietnamese SEA households in this sample are more likely to be earlier arrivals within the five-year time frame than Vietnamese households and to be initially placed in California.

Third, different household types, specifically nuclear and extended households are not significantly different in household size, i.e., the average number of adults and children. However, household composition does vary for these two groups. The number of preschool children, the proportions of households containing preschool child(ren), an infant, or people who are 65 or over are greater in extended households than in nuclear households. These differences are clearer for two different ethnic groups (Vietnamese and non-Vietnamese households) with the exception of the proportion of households containing at least one elderly person. Although the average household size of non-Vietnamese SEA households (6.6 persons) is larger than that of Vietnamese ones (4.8 persons), the average number of adult household members (16 or over) of the first households is smaller than that of the latter. On the other hand, non-Vietnamese refugee households contain more children regardless of age (i.e., ages under one year old, ages from one to five, and from six to fifteen) than Vietnamese refugee households. These differences are statistically significant (p = or < .001).

Fourth, there is no significant difference in the labor force status between household heads and nonhead household members of Southeast Asian refugee households. However, significant differences can be found in the labor force status between nonhead household members of nuclear households and the corresponding household members of extended households. The difference is clearer for Vietnamese refugee households: nonhead household members of extended households show lower rates than their counterparts in nuclear households in terms of labor force participation, work experience since arrival, and employment. These figures posted by nonhead members of extended households can be explained by a significantly greater likelihood of living with preschool children or the elderly, fewer years of schooling in the home country, and fewer number of months spent in the U.S. than those corresponding indices for nonhead members of nuclear households.

Fifth, among nonhead household members, adult children (i.e., unmarried sons and daughters or married sons and daughters) are most likely to be in the labor force and employed. Nonnuclear family members are better off than nuclear family members (i.e. spouses of household heads and other nuclear members such as parents or siblings of the never married household heads) than the adult children in their rates of labor force participation and employment.

The labor force participation and employment rates of nonhead household members are significantly different from those of the household head. Moreover, nonhead household members fare better when their heads are employed. Rates of labor force participation and employment for nonhead household members decrease by half when the heads are unemployed: for labor force participation, from 53 percent to 27 percent, and for employment rate, from 51 percent to 22.5 percent. This trend is stronger for the spouses of the heads. Other nonhead household members such as adult children and nonnuclear family members are less dependent for their labor force status on the employment status of the household heads than wives and husbands of the heads. In particular, adult children of the heads maintain relatively high rates of labor force participation and employment regardless of the employment status of household heads.

Sixth, roughly half of SEA refugee households contain no employed household members. Among the remaining half, about 56 percent have two or more wage-earners and about 46 percent generate only one earner. When nuclear households, extended households, and Vietnamese households are analyzed separately in terms of the wage-earner distribution, they do not differ greatly from the distribution of the households in the whole sample. Non-Vietnamese SEA households, however, are significantly different in the number of wage-earners in the household: roughly eight out of ten non-Vietnamese SEA households have no wage-earners and only four percent of household in this ethnic cohort contain two wage-earners. Therefore, non-Vietnamese SEA households seem to struggle to generate just one earner in the household, not to mention placing one more household member in labor market.

Seventh, when the household pooling of wage labor is decomposed, the presence of adult children as sole or co-earners in the household seems to be very important. Therefore, the husband-wife dual earner model, which is typical of American households, is not as applicable for SEA refugee households. Rather, it is appropriate to say that in general SEA refugee households greatly depend on adult children in generating the first earner (one fifth of all SEA refugee households generating one earner) and multiple earners (about seventy percent of all SEA refugee households generating multiple earners). In addition, one fifth of all SEA refugee households which generate multiple wage-earners depend entirely on two or more adult children for household wage income.

Eighth, the presence of multiple wage-earners in a SEA refugee household is very significant to their use of public assistance and poverty status. More than fifty percent of the SEA refugee households generating two or more wage-earners are off welfare while only 25 percent of one-wage-earner households achieve this result. Also, when the weekly household wage income and the poverty guidelines (for weekly expenses) are considered, only 12 percent of one wage-earner households are above the poverty guidelines, while 84 percent (seven times more) of the multiple-earner households rise above the cutoff point.

Significant factors associated with the generation of multiple wage-earners

First, for the generation of multiple wage-earners among SEA refugee households, all of the three domains of the selected factors (i.e., household structure, human capital of household level, and environmental factors) are found to be important. Among the variables of household structure, except for the number of adult household members, the presence of children and the elderly are significant barriers in the generation of multiple earners in the SEA refugee household. In particular, the presence of preschool children in the household is the most significant negative predictor in that conceptual domain. In the domain of human capital at the household level, the proportion of household members who are currently fluent in English is the most important predictor to increase the odds of being a multiple-earner household. The average years of education for household members is also a significant factor in generating multiple earners in the household. Although less significant, the proportion of prime-aged household members (25-55), and length of English language instruction taken in the home country and the U.S. are positively related to being a multiple-earner household. Also, surprisingly, the SEA refugee households with a shorter time in the U.S. are more likely to generate a multiple number of wage-earners. Among the four selected variables for the domain of refugee households' environments, the proportion of household members who are enrolled in a school, a English language program, or a job-training program, and initial placement in California are very significant factors which decrease the odds of the generation of two or more wage-earners in the Southeast Asian refugee household. The ethnicity of household members and the availability of transportation for household members are not statistically significant for predicting the presence of multiple wage-earners in the Southeast Asian refugee households.

Second, when two additional dependent variables (the generation of the first wage-earner in the household and transition from one-earner households to two or more earner households are included in the logistic regression analyses, significantly different predictors are associated with each of the two dependent variables. In the generation of the first earner in the Southeast Asian refugee household, environmental variables such as the constraint of enrollment in a educational institute (ENROLPER), initial geographical placement (FIRSTST), and household ethnicity (ETHNIC) are significant predictors while none of the variables of household structure are important in accounting for additional wage earners. In contrast, the presence of additional earner(s) in the SEA refugee households is related to only the initial state of resettlement. Instead, household structural variables including number of adult household members, the presence of preschool children, and the presence of elderly are found to be important factors. The proportion of household members who are presently fluent in English is the only human capital variable significantly related to dependent variables. However, this factor becomes more important for generating additional wage-earner(s) than for generating one wage-earner in the SEA refugee household.

Third, when only Vietnamese households are analyzed using logistic regression model, the model is similar to that developed for the whole sample. For non-Vietnamese SEA households, the logistic regression initially could not be conducted due to the small sample sizes of the cohort. Therefore, the independent variables were sorted by their domains (household structure, human capital, and environments) and separate logistic regression analyses were conducted for non-Vietnamese refugee households. In terms of the significance of the environments (such as the initial state of resettlement in the U.S. and the proportion of household members enrolled in an educational institute) on the generation of one earner, this ethnic cohort is not different from the entire sample of Southeast Asian refugee households. However, in contrast to the whole sample, they are significantly influenced by the proportion of male adults in the household and the length of time in the United States since arrival.

DISCUSSION

Extended households and nonnuclear family members

In terms of the wage-earner distribution among Southeast Asian refugee households, extended households are not significantly different from nuclear households: both types of households are about 50 percent no-earner households, close to 20 percent are one-earner households, and roughly 30 percent are multiple-earners households. However, a significant difference was found in the labor force status of nonhead household members (considered as potential secondary earners) between the two types of SEA refugee households. That is, nonhead household members of an extended household are lower than those of a nuclear household in terms of labor force status criteria such as employment, labor force participation, and employment experience since arrival. On first examination, this finding seems to contrast entirely with the experience of immigrants. The research finding of Jensen (1991) was that extended immigrant families received more benefits from secondary earners' (family earners other than the head) contributions than nuclear families.

However, further observation reveals that the gap between two the groups of nonhead household members is due primarily to the significantly lower labor force status of nuclear family members of extended households (e.g., the spouse, child, parent, or sibling of the heads in the extended household) compared to the labor force status of other cohorts of the refugees classified by their family status. For example, 18 percent of the nuclear family members of extended households are employed. This rate of employment is significantly lower than the average rate (34 percent) of all nuclear household members. Compared to any specific family status group of the nuclear household members (i.e., spouse of the head, 23-26 percent; unmarried adult children of the head, 41 percent; siblings or parents of the head,

21 percent), they are still the least likely to be employed. Unlike the nuclear family members of the extended household, the remaining family members of the extended household—nonnuclear family members of the extended household (e.g., married children and their spouse, grandchildren, niece, nephew, or other relatives of the head)— have a close rate of employment (29 percent) to that of nuclear household members (34 percent). They have higher rates than more specific cohorts of family status among the nuclear household members, such as spouse of the head or parents or siblings of the head, except for the unmarried adult children of the head. Therefore, among nonhead household members, the gaps in the labor force status between nuclear and extended households seem to be amplified by a combination of the much lower labor force status of nuclear family members of the extended household and the relatively higher status of unmarried adult children of the nuclear household head.

Therefore, Jensen's (1991) finding has some applicability to SEA refugee households when the more specific family status of the household members is considered because at least nonnuclear family members (54 percent of all nonhead members) of the extended household are more vigorous than the nuclear family members (46 percent of all nonhead members) of the extended household in their wage income generation activities. This trend is similar for Vietnamese refugee and non-Vietnamese SEA refugee households.

The relatively better labor force status of nonnuclear family members in the extended households needs to be considered in terms of the research finding of Angel and Tienda (1982), who studies another immigrant experience of income generation; nonnuclear family members in Hispanic or Black extended households contribute significantly more to the household income compared to non-Hispanic white households in the U.S. Although the extent of the economic contribution of those research populations do not match the level of the labor force status of nonnuclear family members in SEA refugee households, nonnuclear family members among SEA refugees seems to correspond to the immigrant or racial minority cohort in terms of their significant economic contribution to the household.

Overall, the significant economic advantage of extended households found in prior research does not match the findings of the current study. If there is a finding of the current study corresponding to the prior ones, it would be the relatively more vigorous labor force participation and better employment status of nonnuclear family members of extended households than the spouses of the head in the nuclear family households. This relatively better status of nonnuclear family members in extended households, however, is diluted by the very low employment and labor force participation rates of other members of extended households (i.e., nuclear family members in extended households) and by the impressive labor force status of adult children in the nuclear households.

Role of adult children

In fact, the discussion of the potential economic benefits of an extended household has been driven by the trend that immigrant or Southeast Asian refugee households resettled in the United States contain a relatively high proportion of extended family households compared to American family households. Therefore, among these extended households, significant economic contributions by nonhead household members (Jensen's study) or nonnuclear family members (Angel and Tienda's study) can be a means for enhancing the economic status of those households to a considerable extent. However, the distribution of household types for the data of recently arrived Southeast Asian refugees in the present study indicates that the proportion (10.5 percent) of extended households is not very great. Also, the labor force status of extended household members is not better than that of the nuclear household members. Rather, the most notable findings of the present study are that nuclear households predominate (about 84 percent) among Southeast Asian refugee households and that the adult children in the nuclear household, who are found to be significantly more active in the labor force participation and more successful in employment than any other family members, comprise the major group (about 56 percent) among nonhead household members.

The meaning of the relatively successful labor force status of the adult children (especially those in nuclear households) is clarified when the household heads are unemployed. Although, like other nonhead household members, the labor force participation and employment status of adult children of the heads are dependent on their head's employment status, they are more likely to be in the labor force or employed when their heads are employed then when the heads are not. However, adult children are the cohort which is the least dependent on the employment status of the household head. This means that when the household head is unemployed the adult children are still the most likely to be in the labor force and be employed. This is more clear when comparing the employment rate of wives of the household heads (32 percent of all nonhead household members) to that of the adult children of the household heads (51 percent of all nonhead household members). When the head is employed, the adult children (55 percent) are slightly higher in their employment rate than the wives (51 percent). However, when the head is not employed, the employment rate of the wives drops drastically (to 6.5 percent) while that of the adult children drops moderately (to 33 percent). This trend in the employment rate is very similar to that of the labor force participation rate. Therefore, adult children are as important as spouses as potential additional wage-earners when the household heads are already generating wage income. Adult children are also very important as likely substitutes for the household head in the role of income generation among all household members.

The fact that the labor force status of nonhead household members' is very dependent on the employment status of the household head may indicate that the head and nonhead members in the household have very similar characteristics, such as similar human capital. If this is true, the similarity in the human capital is expected to be stronger between heads and the spouses of the heads than between heads and adult children because the labor force status (labor force participation and employment) of the spouses is more likely to be the same as the employment status of the head than is the status of other nonhead members (especially of adult children).

To test these expectations, ad hoc analyses were conducted examining the similarity in years of education and current English fluency between the head and the spouse and between the head and the adult children. As expected, the spouses have relatively similar human capital to that of the household heads. Moreover, employed heads and their spouses are, on the average, more educated (10 years and 9 years, respectively) than unemployed heads and their spouses (8 years and 7 years, respectively). Also, the employed heads and their spouses had, on the average, more fluency in English at the time of interview (2.6 and 2.9, respectively) than unemployed heads and their spouses (3.0 and 3.2, respectively. A lower value means better fluency). However, as also expected, adult children are not as similar to household heads in their level of human capital. When the head is employed, the average years of education of the heads and their adult children are the same (about 10 years), but when the head is unemployed, the head's average is about 8 years and the children's is about 10 years. If the similarity in human capital found among the spouses and the household heads would extend to the adult children, the average years of education of the children should be as low as that of the unemployed heads (i.e., should be closer to 8 years). However, their education years are consistent regardless of the employment status of their household heads (i.e., mostly considered as their parents). Also, the adult children are, on the average, more fluent in English than household heads regardless of the employment status of the heads (2.3 vs. 2.6 when their head is employed and 2.5 vs. 3.0 when the head is unemployed). These statistics provide a clue to explaining the much greater labor force status of adult children of the heads among SEA refugee households. That is, their consistently better human capital, which is almost equal to or sometimes better than that of household heads, seems to be, one of the very important factors which make them enter to the labor market and be able to be employed either when the head is employed or not employed. Therefore, the adult children are the major secondary earners along with the spouses of the heads (mostly, wives) in SEA refugee households. Also, they are the major source of alternate sole wage-earner(s) with considerably more propensity to be employed than the wives of household heads (32 percent, compared to adult children at 51 percent).

The findings from the decomposition of household wage-earners confirm the points discussed above. Among the households which generate only one earner who is a nonhead household member, about 60 percent depend on adult children for household wage income. The remaining 40 percent indicate the households which have only one earner who is a spouse of the head. For the SEA refugee households which contain multiple number of wage-earners, 25 percent of them depend only on their adult children for household wage income. These cases refer to the SEA refugee households in which the head is unemployed and only adult children are fulfilling the role of the head's household income generation. Also, the proportion of multiple-earner households which contain adult children as wage-earners is 70 percent, while the households in which the spouses of the heads are participating in the household wage labor organization comprise about 50 percent of the entire sample. These trends were found to be very similar when only nuclear households were analyzed.

The reason for repeating the decomposing work for nuclear households was to include only never-married children, who are expected to be younger than the married adult children in the extended households, and examine whether the unmarried adult children are significantly important for the household wage labor generation among the SEA refugee population. In terms of magnitude, nuclear households are the dominant (about 84 percent) household type among the SEA refugee household sample and the adult children in the nuclear households are also the dominating group (91 percent) of all adult children of the household head. Among all sons and daughters, about 35 percent are 25 or over and one in ten unmarried adult children is 30 or over. These frequencies are the same for those in the nuclear households. Roughly one out of two nuclear family households contains at least one unmarried adult child who is 25 or over and one of five contain at least one adult child who is 30 or over. SEA refugee households contain as many as seven unmarried adult children.

The age distribution of unmarried adult children is similar for sons and daughters. Also, the age of those adult children and their employment status are positively correlated (Pearson correlation coefficient, $r = .29$, $p < .000$). This relationship continues even when their years of education and current English fluency are controlled ($r = .26$, $p < .000$). In contrast, the ages of household members other than those unmarried adult children have a negative relationship to the employment status when education and English fluency are controlled ($r = -.09$, $p < .01$) or not ($r = -.07$, $p < .05$).

The final evidence for the importance of the presence of unmarried adult children is that the proportion of the unmarried adult children among all household members in a nuclear household is positively correlated with the number of wage-earners in the household. Among the nuclear households which contain no or only one earner, the proportion of unmarried adult children is almost the same as that of the spouses of household heads (about 30 percent). However, among the nuclear households which generate two or more earners the proportion (54 percent) of the adult children is more than twice that (21 percent) of spouses of the head. These distributions of adult children in nuclear households confirm that their presence in the Southeast Asian refugee households is very important for the generation of multiple earners.

Therefore, we can conclude that relatively older adult children (in general from 25 to 40, therefore, considered as those who are in the prime age range, 25-45), who comprise about 30 percent of all unmarried adult children, are living with their parent(s) and that accordingly, can contribute economically to the household by increasing the probability of a multiple-earner household through pooling their wage labor with others', such as the head and/or the spouse of the head, or their relatively younger brothers or sisters. Actually, these relatively older unmarried adult children may be individuals who generally would have married and created independent nuclear family households. If they had done so, the proportion of nuclear households would be larger and the proportion of dual wage-earners (husband and wife) might be greater. If these individuals married and remained in their parental households, the proportion of extended households would be greater and nonnuclear family members (when the unmarried adult children marry and do not leave their families) in the extended household would appear to make a more impressive contribution to household labor force participation and employment status. The first case is close to a typical American style while the latter case is similar to that of immigrants in the United States. However, by not getting married (perhaps due to the seriousness of economic problems in the environments surrounding themselves and their family) and staying with their families, the relatively old adult children in nuclear households seem to be the significant variable that characterizes the household wage labor organization among SEA refugee households.

Adult children vs. household heads and their spouses

It is also interesting that household head or the spouse of the heads are not as much restrained by the presence of children as are other adult household members (especially unmarried adult children). In terms of their employment status being less influenced by the presence of children, heads (primarily men adults) and spouse of the heads (primarily wives) are not different when the years of education and English fluency are controlled. For both cohorts, correlation coefficients are $-.08$ and these results are statistically significant($p <$ $.05$). It can be interpreted that the heads and their spouses are less competitive than the adult children group (regardless of household type) because of their poorer quality of human capital. (In general, education years and current English fluency were analyzed for representing human capital). Therefore, their employment status, which is restrained by the low level of human capital, is relatively uninfluenced by the presence of children compared to adult children. This trend becomes clearer when only female heads or wives of household heads are analyzed and compared to daughters. While the daughters have very similar levels of years of education and English fluency as those for the sons, the wives and female heads are considerably poorer in those kinds of human capital than male heads or husbands of household heads. Therefore, the fact that these female heads and spouses (i.e., wives, mothers, or female heads) stay out of the labor force due primarily to lack of their human capital appears to be an influential factor in the relatively weak relationship between labor force status and presence of children, which implicates the burden of family care.

On the other hand, the employment status of adult children was the most likely to be influenced by the presence of children in the household ($r = -.23$, p=.0000, when the years of education and current English fluency were controlled) among all household members. The constraint on employment by child care seems to be greater for daughters ($r = -.32$) than for sons ($r = -.11$). Also, the duty seems to pose a more serious constraint for relatively older (e.g., 21 or older, $r = -.20$) than for relatively younger adult children (e.g., 20 or younger, $r = -.11$).

The employment status of the adult children is, on the other hand, less related to their human capital than household heads and the spouses of the heads. When the presence of children in the household is controlled, the length of education and current English fluency are not significantly related to employment status. These trends are not much different between sons and daughters for the cohort of adult children. In contrast, the employment of heads and spouses of the heads is significantly influenced by the years of education ($r = .19$, p =.000) and current English fluency ($r = .24$, p = .000) when the presence of children is controlled.

Non-Vietnamese SEA households in the wage-earner generation

In the distribution of the number of wage-earners in the household, another notable finding emerges from ethnic comparison (Vietnamese and non-Vietnamese SEA households). Non-Vietnamese SEA households, strikingly contrasted with Vietnamese ones, are primarily no-earner households (82 percent), rarely (4 percent) multiple-earner households. As pointed out in the earlier section, non-Vietnamese SEA households seem to struggle to produce just one wage-earner in the household. The significantly lower probability of generation of multiple earners in non-Vietnamese SEA households can be seen as an extension of the poorer labor force status of individual non-Vietnamese refugees. Also, just like the relatively poor human capital of individuals has been explained by prior studies as a major reason for the poorer labor market outcomes for non-Vietnamese SEA refugees (Potocky and McDonald, 1995; Rumbaut, 1989), several kinds of household-level human capital of non-Vietnamese SEA refugee households seem to be significant factors in determining the lower probability of generating wage-earner(s) in the household. However, the present study shows that, in addition to the household-level human capital, different household composition can be another significant factor which explains ethnic differences in the wage-earner-generation capability of the households. Specifically, fewer adult household members and considerably more children who are under 17 can be important explanatory factors for the significantly lower capability of wage-earner generation of non-Vietnamese SEA refugee households.

The significant factors for wage-earner generation.

The results of logistic regression analyses for Southeast Asian refugee households reflect the results of analyzing individual household members for their labor force status and the facilitators or constraints for the status. The importance of household structure (presence of children) for the adult children and human capital variables (education years and current English fluency) for household heads and the spouses of the heads seems to be reflected in the independent variables, which were found to be relatively important factors associated with being a multiple-earner household. Also, both the two cohorts (adult children and household heads and their spouses) have disadvantages in their labor force status from the fact that they were initially placed in California and that they are currently enrolled in an educational program or a school. These factors were also found to be very important factors in multiple-earner generation among Southeast Asian refugee households. Therefore, to explain the increase in the probability of being a multiple-earner household is not possible from one domain of selected variables because the given dependent variable is a result of the combination of the wage labor of individual household members, whose individual characteristics and experiences of resettlement in the U.S. could be different according to their family status.

It is also interesting that different factors are associated with two different dependent variables (the generation of first earner in the household, ONEEMP, and the generation of additional earners, ADDITIONAL). In differentiating the one wage-earner households from no wage-earner households, the variables in the domain of household structure and the ones in the domain of household-level human capital are relatively unimportant. However, in differentiating multiple wage-earner households from the one wage-earner households, the variables of household structure and human capital of household members are more important. Specifically, the presence of preschool children and the proportion of household members who are fluent in English at time of the interview are significantly related to the generation of more than one wage-earner. Therefore, child-care responsibility and household-level of English language fluency seem to play relatively important roles in the generation of one more earner in a SEA refugee household as a significant constraint and a facilitator, respectively.

In contrast, the importance of two environmental factors which were found to be constraints for generation of the first wage-earner, CALIFORNIA and ENROLPER, seem to fade out when they are used in the logistic regression for different variables, that is, the generation of additional earners. Therefore, it is believed that the generation of additional earners relies more on household structure and human capital than on such environmental constraints as the state in which refugees are initially resettled (as a proxy of current residential area) or enrollment in training programs or a school.

The finding that the households which were initially placed in California are worse off in the generation of earners (both one and additional earners) seems to be an extension of the findings of prior studies which reported the relatively low labor force status of individual SEA refugees who are living in California. In fact, as mentioned before, the initial placement state is an alternative to the current residence area (state). However, due to the limitation of data, information about the initial state was employed while ignoring the possibility of interstate-secondary migrations after initial resettlement. However, this alternative variable was still found to be very significant.

The Californian SEA households are significantly poorer than the SEA refugee households resettled in other states, even after controlling for many possibly related factors (i.e., the independent variables included in the logistic regression model). In fact, the first cohort is not statistically different in many variables of human capital of household level. Also, although there is a minor difference in the likelihood of children between the two household cohorts, this difference results primarily from the fact that a greater proportion of non-Vietnamese SEA households, which are known to contain on the average more children in the household than Vietnamese households, were initially placed in California (22 percent) than in the other states (14 percent). Therefore, when the ethnicity of households (Vietnamese or non-Vietnamese) was controlled, most of the differences related to the presence or number of children in the household disappear. The only factor which still remains to differentiate non-Vietnamese SEA households initially placed in California from their counterparts resettled in the other states is the number of preschool children. On the average, Californian non-Vietnamese SEA households contain 1.9 preschool children and their counterparts about 1.3 preschool children. Based on these findings, relatively low employment rates for Californian male and female adults, in particular for female adults, could be said to result from the greater number of preschool children and accordingly heavier load of child care than the household members initially resettled in other states. However, because this difference was limited only to non-Vietnamese SEA households whose proportion is small (about 17 percent of all SEA refugee households), it is still not clear why household members initially placed in California showed poorer employment status than household members resettled in the other states. However, further investigation of this issue is warranted but is beyond the scope of this paper.

The number of adults in the household (not including high school students) is not related to the generation of one or two wage-earners in the household, but very influential in generating more than two wage-earners in the household. If the generation of two wage-earners in a SEA refugee household could mean a minimally enough level of household economy for the refugee population, the number of adults (on the average, 3 to 3.5) would not be an influential factor in creating dual earners in the Southeast Asian refugee households which contain at least two adults who are not high school students.

The presence of the elderly was found to be another constraint in the generation of multiple earners in the Southeast Asian refugee household, although this factor is only significant when accepting a more liberal criterion (i.e., p < .10). This factor seems to have two ways of constraining the occurrence of multiple earners: first, their presence means a decrease in the number of more employable adult household members (e.g., young or prime-aged household members); second, their presence means an increase in the family-care duty for other household members and consequently constrains them from entering the labor market.

The average weeks of English language instruction taken in the home country and in the United States are almost same in the relative importance for predicting the generation of multiple wage-earners among Southeast Asian refugee households. In order to know which of the two kinds of English language education (in the home country or in the U.S.) more influenced current fluency in English, correlation analyses were conducted while controlling ethnicity. The results indicate that the current level of English language ability is influenced by these two kinds of English language education to almost the same extent (Pearson correlation coefficient, r = .094 and r = .095). The average years of education of a household or the length of time in the United States. have a relatively strong relationship to the proportion of fluent household members (r = .24 and r = .20, respectively). These findings are true when those relationships are examined for individual refugees rather than households.

Although it is significant only when p is equal to or less than .10, the length of time in the U.S., surprisingly, was not helpful in enhancing the household economic situation. More specifically, the Southeast Asian refugee households which arrived early have less probability of being a multiple-earner household than those households which arrived later within the five year time frame. This situation can be due partly to the ethnic distribution of Southeast Asian refugee households. In general, among the households in this sample, Vietnamese households, which are regarded as generally higher in the labor force status and more likely to produce multiple wage-earners, arrived later than non-Vietnamese SEA refugees[1]. Therefore, when all ethnic cohorts of SEA refugee households are included in the analysis, the time of arrival seems to influence the relationship between the time in the U.S. and the probability of generating multiple wage-earners in a household. However, when the ethnicity of the household is controlled, in the generation of multiple earners in the household Vietnamese households are still negatively influenced by the length of the time in the U.S. (p < .10). In contrast, non-Vietnamese SEA refugee households, as shown in the logistic regression results, benefit from longer living in the U.S. for generating one earner in the household. The average length of job training taken by household members is not a predictor for the generation of multiple number of wage-earners.

For reference, the employment rate of job training participants (individual refugees) is 41 percent while that of nonparticipants is 35 percent. This difference in the rates is not statistically significant. One more notable thing about job training is that the proportion of the household members who took the training is very small (about 6 percent of all adults). This proportion of job training participants is considerably low compared to that for English language trainees (about 53 percent). These findings seem to confirm the comments by the prior documents about SEA refugees' economic adjustment. Hing (1993)argues, most refugees cannot acquire "the skills that would qualify them for anything other than minimum wage jobs in 18 months." (p. 137) Moreover, lack of opportunity for job training has already been pointed out. After investigation about employment problems of Southeast Asian refugee in 1982, General Accounting Office found that "[Southeast Asian] refugees wanted jobs and job training but [found] lack of adequate counseling or sufficient access to [employment] programs" and that only 14 percent of the employable age refugees were able to be employed during the resettlement time (Kerpen 1985:23-24). Another study (Caplan et al. 1990) of SEA refugee also indicated ineffectiveness of vocational training for Southeast Asian refugees. Although "there is a positive and statistically significant [. . .] relationship between vocational training and being off cash assistance(p. 218)", According to the study, the quality of the jobs which those who were trained in the vocational training program was not much different from those who did not use vocational training.

Due to very few cases of multiple-earner households, small size of the sample, and relatively many of independent variables, non-Vietnamese SEA households were analyzed by the three separate logistic regression models, each of which contain only one domain of the initially selected independent variables. The results indicate that non-Vietnamese SEA households are similar to Vietnamese ones in that they are influenced by the initial place of resettlement and the proportion of household members who are enrolled in a school of a educational program but not by the presence of children and current English. However, unlike Vietnamese refugee households, they are positively influenced by the proportion of male adults (in the domain of household structure) and by the length of time in the United States since arrival (in the domain of household-level of human capital). The first variable, the proportion of male adult household members, is indicative of the fact that female household members in the non-Vietnamese SEA households have a bigger gap than male adults in terms of employment rates than their counterparts cohort in Vietnamese households. However, a more notable finding here is that non-Vietnamese SEA household members, regardless of gender, have a very low employment rate compared to Vietnamese; while Vietnamese household males and females are 43 percent and 33 percent, respectively, non-Vietnamese SEA refugee household males and females are 15 percent and 5 percent, respectively. The relationship to 'the length of stay in the United States' shows that the prior finding of the positive relationship between the labor force status and the length of time in the United States seems to repeat, not for Vietnamese, but for non-Vietnamese SEA refugee households only. When the correlation between the length of time in the United States and the number of workers in the household was examined while controlling for the number of adult household members in a household, the presence or absence of children under age 17, and the proportion of household members who are currently fluent in English, Vietnamese households showed no significant relationship (Pearson correlation coefficient, $r = .02$) while in the generation of one wage-earner ($r = .26$) non-Vietnamese refugee households was much influenced by the length of the time in the United States. Therefore, the advantage of longer lived households for the generation of wage-earner(s) seems to be applied to only non-Vietnamese refugee households within the time frame of the initial 5 years since arrival. However, these regression analyses results for non-Vietnamese SEA households are still limited to generalization and comparison to those for Vietnamese refugee households primarily because of the size of the sample.

The relationship among multiple earner, public assistance, and poverty

Although Southeast Asian refugee households, by generating multiple wage-earners, can significantly increase the proportion of welfare-independent households (up to 52 percent) and the proportion of households out of poverty (up to 84 percent), the remaining proportions of households for each of the indicators are still dependent on public assistance or are below the poverty lines. The finding that, despite the presence of two or more earners, about 48 percent of Southeast Asian refugee households are still dependent on at least one kind of public assistance can be an indicator of their insufficient wage income for living. This conviction is also based on the proportion of such households which are below the poverty lines indicated in chapter four (refer to table 4.11). The proportion in poverty was calculated by comparing the total weekly household wage income to the minimum living costs for a week guided by poverty lines (per family). Therefore, the comparison assumes that the wage-earners earn the presented amount of weekly wage income for 52 weeks a year. However, actually the wage-earners of SEA refugee households work on the average about 37 weeks a year. Only about 55 percent of the workers answered that they worked more than 48 weeks during the "last year." Therefore, the comparison of weekly household wage income to the poverty lines can be an overestimation for Southeast Asian refugee household economic conditions.

Despite this overestimation, about 16 percent of the Southeast Asian refugee households are still below the poverty lines. If we can get a correct estimation for the annual household wage income, probably this proportion would increase. This situation indicates that, for some proportion of multiple-earner SEA households, the additional wage income generated by the secondary earner(s) is not enough to overcome the economic plight of the households. Therefore, the use of public assistance by those multiple earners should not be regarded as welfare dependency, rather it must be understood as an effort to compensate for the gap between their earned income and the costs needed for a minimum level of living.

This issue was also mentioned by Bach and Argiros (1991), who suggested that the matter of public aid dependency by Southeast Asian refugees should be understood in the context of the problems of the working poor. According to their research, among the cash payment recipients of Southeast Asian refugees, a large proportion reflect refugee households which have two income sources, from earned income and cash benefits. These are considered the working poor, who are "caught in the middle of the mismatch between entry level wages in part related to low minimum-wage rates, payment levels of public assistance programs, and a standard of living deemed minimal by the federal government" (Bach and Argiros, 1991, p. 340). In fact, the average wage rate for Southeast Asian refugees in the current study is $6.08 and about 12 percent of them were receiving the minimum wage ($ 4.25) or less. This low wage situation seems to be a major reason why about 25 percent of two-earner households are below the poverty lines even when assuming they work 52 weeks per year. The fact that many are also under-employed (Majka and Mullan, 1992) means that their economic situation is worse than estimated here.

NOTES

1. The table presents the distribution of Vietnamese and non-Vietnamese SEA households by the length (year) of time in the United States.

Length of time	Vietnamese households	Non-Vietnamese SEA households
0 -12 months	11.4 %	6.0%
13 -24 months	22.3%	12.5%
25 -36 months	20.7%	20.0%
37 -48 months	20.5%	18.5%
49 -66 months	25.1%	42.9%

CHAPTER 6

Practice and Research Implications

POLICY AND PRACTICE IMPLICATIONS

The importance of the presence of adult children in the generation of a multiple-earner household naturally implies that policies and actual services of Southeast Asian refugee resettlement in the United States should stress ways to strengthen their labor force participation and employability.

Adult children are found to be higher than their parents (especially for nuclear households which constitute 84 percent of the sample) in human capital such as years of education and English fluency. Although on the average, the adult children's employment was not found to be influenced by such human capital as education level and current English ability, those adult children in the no-earner and one-earner SEA refugee households have poorer human capital than those in the multiple-earner households. Therefore, to invest in enhancing the human capital of those adult children who are not in the labor force or are unemployed would be an effective way to create the first earner in the no-earner household and to generate additional wage-earner(s) in the one-earner household. Furthermore, the finding that the adult children of SEA refugee households are not significantly influenced by education level and English language ability does not mean that it is not necessary to invest human capital for those adult children. Reflecting that their employment rates (about 45 percent) are still lower than the averages of other ethnic refugee populations such as Latin Americans (57 percent) or Eastern Europeans (53 percent) (ORR, 1995), they stand to benefit from enhanced human capital.

Also, further human capital investments for those adult children can be an effective way of enhancing their employment quality (e.g., retention of a job, a full-time job, higher wage rates, etc.). Better quality of employment can increase the extent of independence from welfare by increasing the amount of household wage income among multiple-earner SEA refugee households.

This emphasis on human capital development must also be applied to the heads and their spouses because another major part of the composition of multiple earners is related to these household members. Investments in human capital may be needed more for the household heads and their spouses (for the nuclear household, they are the parents of the adult children) than the adult children in that their employment status is found to be much influenced by such human capital factors as previous education and English fluency. In general, the heads and their spouses were found to be similar in educational background and English fluency, and accordingly, the spouses are more likely to be in the labor force and employed if the heads are working. Therefore, in the case of households with an unemployed head, the households are very likely to be no-earner households unless adult children are present and can be an alternative source of wage income. In fact, when the heads and their spouses do not have the adult children in the nuclear household (this type of nuclear households comprises about 40 percent of all nuclear households), they are more likely to be no-earner households compared to all nuclear households. Also, the employment rates of those heads and their spouses are not much different from those rates of the heads and the spouses who are living with adult children. That means, even though adult children are not present in the household and there is no alternative source of wage income, these couples cannot participate more vigorously in the labor market because of their fundamental lack of human capital. Therefore, the married couple or parents in this type of nuclear household need to be especially assisted by education and training for them to enter the labor market and be employed.

The average age of the cohort of the heads and their spouses is about 44 years old, which is the same for those in nuclear and extended households. Reflecting on the average age for the relatively old household members (primarily household heads and their spouses), more specific job training seems to be needed which can enhance their skill transferability. Specific job training means broadly "remedial education" rather than teaching a new skill. The most critical basic remedial education for Southeast Asian refugees is English language training. Other basic skills must be developed as well. In addition, Southeast Asian refugees need basic knowledge and information about potential occupations or workplaces and skills related to job search. Current programs which encompass "general orientation to the American job market and workplace practice" (Caplan et al., 1990, p. 216) should be continued.

The federal office , i.e., Office of Refugee Resettlement, requires states with welfare utilization rates at 55 percent or higher to use at least 85 percent of funds for social service for the "priority services such as English language training, employment counseling, job placement, vocational training. and employment related service" (ORR, 1995, p. 24). Thus, the emphasis of the ORR's policies is on encouraging rapid achievement of self-sufficiency. The remaining 15 percent of the funds for social services are spent for "orientation, translation, social adjustment, transportation, and day care" (ORR, 1995, p. 24). Also, most of the "target assistance" programs by federal government's discretionary grant concentrate on English or vocational training and employment services to promote early self-sufficiency of refugees.

Despite the emphasis on employment assistance in refugee resettlement programs, the results of this study (i.e., the logistic regression analyses) indicate that the average number of weeks of job training for household members was not found to be effective for increasing number of wage-earners, regardless of the different dependent variables examined, or ethnicity of the Southeast Asian refugee households (Vietnamese and non-Vietnamese). According to the basic statistics reported by the ORR, only 5.6 percent of Vietnamese and 5.3 percent of other Southeast Asian refugees have participated in job training since they arrived in the United States. When a correlation test for employment status and the weeks of job training for all the participants was conducted, there was no significant relationship between the length of job training and being employed. Also, the SEA refugees who have participated in job training are not more likely to be employed than those who have not. These findings indicate that there must a discrepancy between policy direction and actual practices, both of which aim at increasing refugees' employability and that there must be more detailed evaluation of the job training process for the refugee.

Provision of alternative child care can increase the proportion of multiple earner households particularly by allowing the adult children to enter the labor market. The benefit will be greater for female adult children than males because the first cohort is constrained more than two times as much by the presence of children as the latter. In the child-containing SEA refugee households, adult daughters were found to be more influenced by the presence of children than female heads or wives of the household heads. This fact indicates that if familial or institutional child care is not secured, employment of the young women who are generally not married and the adult daughters, who have relatively high rates of labor force participation and employment along with the sons of household heads, significantly drop and in turn, the probability of generating multiple wage-earners can decrease among the child-containing households.

The presence of the elderly is found to discourage the generation of multiple wage-earners in Southeast Asian refugee households. One of the initial expectations about the role of the elderly was that they could fulfill the role of caring for children in the household and accordingly contribute to the household economy by letting other household members, particularly the mother of the children or adult children enter the labor market. However, their presence, on the contrary, plays a negative role in increasing wage-earners in the household. When both young children and the elderly are present in the household, other family members in the household are significantly impaired in their employment compared to those in the households which contain only child(ren). This trend is true for men and women, and stronger for the women (dropping in the employment rate from 20 percent to 8 percent) than men (from 32 percent to 26 percent). Therefore, institutional care or other facilities for the care of the elderly must also be arranged along with child care.

The research finding that the trend of multiple earner generation is very different according to ethnicity of the household provides a significant implication for the policy planners and resettlement practitioners. Briefly, the policies and practices of refugee assistance for generating multiple earners in the SEA refugee household have to be ethnically oriented. Particularly when we divide the SEA refugee households into two ethnic groups (i.e., Vietnamese and non-Vietnamese), the resettlement assistance policy has to focus more on the first ethnic cohort than the second cohort because non-Vietnamese SEA refugee households are struggling to generate the first earner in the household. In general, non-Vietnamese SEA refugees have been known to be poorer in human capital compared to their Vietnamese counterparts. They also, on the average, have a different household structure from that of Vietnamese refugees. Although these differences between two ethnic groups of Southeast Asian refugees have been discussed in prior research, these have to be reconsidered for the household analyses, such as household labor organization, and for the policy planning of increasing wage-earners in the ethnic groups.

As noted in the earlier chapters, the Southeast Asian refugee households first resettled in California are significantly poorer than their counterparts households in the generation of wage-earners, although this trend seems to lessen in the case of generating two or more wage-earners. Those Californian households are also more likely to use at least one kind of public assistance than non-Californian SEA refugee households (83 percent vs. 66 percent, respectively). Although, the reasons for these facts were not discussed fully in this paper and are still unclear, previous work has examined this issue. According to Bach and Argiros (1991), the disparity between California and other states in the economic and labor force status of Southeast Asian refugee households can be explained by three points: 1) the history of the resettlement experience, 2) the demographic and household composition of the refugee population, and 3) the conditions in local labor markets. The first point means that California has more generous public assistance policy directions for the refugees than other states and the second indicates that relatively complex family compositions and the large size of the Californian households make them more likely to be eligible for assistance programs. The discussion of the first point may be very complicated because it is also related to the very fundamental issues of welfare receipt and work motivation, especially for the refugee households corresponding the non-working poor. It is still unclear and needs additional research.

The second recommendation could fit the current sample of Californian refugee households because they are more likely to be larger in household size and to contain more children than are those resettled in other states. However, this situation results partly from the disproportional distribution of ethnicity of Southeast Asian refugee households: more non-Vietnamese SEA households, which contain on the average considerably more children, resettled in California than Vietnamese ones.

The third suggestion is actually beyond the scope of this book to fully explain. However, evidences from data analysis suggest that conditions in the local (i.e., California) labor market may be very limited, providing insufficient earnings due to low wages, for Southeast Asian refugees. The refugee workers resettled in California, in addition to this lower employment rate, are paid significantly less than their counterparts resettled in other states. The average hourly wage for the Californian refugees is $5.48, compared to refugees in other states who earn on average, $6.31 per hour. This trend is the same for the heads and their spouses and for the adult children cohort. As a result, their weekly household wage incomes are also lower than those of non-Californians. Economic disadvantages of the Southeast Asian refugee household members in California may be due to the greater competition for jobs because of presence of the workers from other immigrant pools (for example, migrant workers from Mexico). According to recent reports of the Office of Refugee Resettlement, a great number of the initial and the secondary placements has resulted in high density of refugee populations in large urban areas or metropolitan cities in California, Texas, Florida, and New York. Many of the secondary refugee migrants as well as newly arrived refugees seems to experience intense competition with other unemployed workers in the areas (Kerpen, 1985).

Finally, the fact that even half of the multiple-earner households are relying on public assistance and some of them cannot rise about the poverty level is a rationale for continued public assistance programs for the Southeast Asian refugee households. In this case, the meaning of assisting working poor refugees is to "compensate for the hardships encountered inside the labor market" (Bach and Argiros, 1991, p. 342). For example, employment in secondary sector jobs typically provides low wages, no fringe benefits, and underemployment. Bach and Argiros (1991) stress that such households that need access to both earned and transfer income are those for which resettlement policy and "programs alone, including private, voluntary sponsorship, may be ill-prepared." They suggest that the cause and the solution to the problem of working poor refugees is to be found in a broader social context, in which the problem of the working poor is more seriously considered. For example, "congressional debate on the working poor . . . often focuses on reforms such as increases in the federal minimum wage and retraining assistance" (Bach and Argiros, 1991, p. 342) have direct benefits for the refugee population too. Here, too the issues of local labor markets experienced by Southeast Asian refugees and investment in human capital for them warrants further consideration.

LIMITATION OF THE STUDY

One of the limitations of this paper is that it dose not address the demand aspect of refugees' labor, which refers to employers' attitudes about refugees' labor, information on the local and nation-wide labor market situation, and even ethnic enclave labor markets of Southeast Asian refugees. These factors have frequently been discussed for the general U.S. workers and other ethnic groups (Dickens and Lang, 1985; Dickens and Lang, 1993; Light, Sabagh, Bozorgmehr, and Der-Martirosian, 1994; Wilson and Portes, 1980). These factors are essential elements of information about the destination country and need to be studied to better understand the refugees' economic adjustment. Social, cultural, and personal characteristics of refugees and how they related to the assistance programs that exist to serve them is also valuable (Haines, 1989).

Lack of a large sample of extended households and non-Vietnamese SEA households limited the use of logistic regression results for these cohorts of SEA refugee households. Although for non-Vietnamese SEA households, three separate logistic regression analyses were conducted for a dependent variable (i.e., the generation of first one wage-earner in a household), a more correct comparison for the two large divisions of ethnic cohorts (Vietnamese and non-Vietnamese SEA refugee households) requires the application of the same regression model for both cohorts. Also, more sizable data for these relatively small-size groups of Southeast Asian refugee households would provide clearer results for the descriptions of household and individual characteristics and for basic comparison work.

In the descriptive statistics, weekly household wage incomes were compared to the official poverty guidelines. Because the annual incomes from wage labor for individual refugees were not appropriate for use because of too many missing values, this study employed the weekly incomes to estimate the extent of poverty of the household. When this study compare the sum of weekly wages for all household members to official poverty lines, there is a gap between two concepts; poverty guidelines are set for a year and weekly incomes are for only a week. Therefore, the annual amounts of minimum living costs set for the poverty guidelines were divided by 52 (i.e., number of weeks in a year) in order to obtain the poverty level for a week and to compare the weekly wage incomes of the household. At this time, the poverty status of households reflects only the wage income conditions during a particular week. This is an inevitable limitation of this research due to lack of information about the annual incomes for the individual refugees. Also, although data were available about the number of weeks worked last year and earnings before taxes during the last 12 months, these variables could not be used because they also contained too many missing cases (approximately 40 percent and 70 percent for all applicable cases, respectively). On the basis only of non-missing cases, the average number of weeks SEA refugees worked in 1993-1994 is 37 weeks (median 49 weeks). Therefore, when the time period is not a week but a year, the proportions of households which are above the poverty guidelines may need to be adjusted (downward) reflecting the fact that SEA refugee individuals on the average work much less than 52 weeks a year.

RECOMMENDATIONS FOR FUTURE RESEARCH

The contents of this book provide numerous additional topics for future studies, including comparison work in the household labor organization and wage-earner generation. Additional ethnic comparisons may yield interesting results. Specifically, refugees from Eastern European countries, who are primarily Jewish immigrants from the former Soviet Union, are known to have very different household compositions from Southeast Asian refugees and be higher in their economic and labor force status than the research population for the present paper (ORR, 1995). A study (Gold, 1988) was conducted for the comparison of those two ethnic cohorts of refugees on the areas of small business and self-employment. Also, Pfeffer (1994) compared Cambodian farm workers to African-American ones in Philadelphia. These ethnic comparison may be able to expand to the areas of household wage labor composition for those ethnic or racial cohorts. How do they adjust to their economic situations in the United States? What are their major types of household labor composition? How are they different from those of Southeast Asian refugees? These questions can be asked and the studies can expand to other ethnic groups of refugees in the United States such as refugees from Latin

America and the Middle East. Since the original data has information about all ethnic refugee groups in the United States, these ethnic comparisons can be possible without a further data collection. Further comparison work can be done on the basis of length of time in the United States. This book, as mentioned in the earlier chapter, covers only the refugee households that have spent up to about 5 years in the United States since their arrival. Future study could expand to Southeast Asian refugee households that have spent more than 5 years in the United States. Such research can shed light on how multiple-earner generation strategies vary between the initial resettlement period (within 5 years after arrival) and the later period.

Further analyses are also needed to explore the geographical differences (for example, California and nonCalifornia states) in the labor force status of individual refugees and of household level. Why are the Southeast Asian households resettled in California worse than residents of other state in their economic and labor force status? Although this topic was mentioned briefly in the present paper, more detailed and more systematic studies are needed. Do other ethnic cohorts of refugees have similar trends in labor force status according to geographical location? Particularly, welfare policy and local labor market conditions seem to be important issues that eventually must be discussed. In addition, future research should address other structural factors such as the formation of ethnic enclaves for the Southeast Asian refugees. Moreover, what role do they play in the generation of wage-income or of multiple-earners in the households. How might SEA refugee ethnic enclaves influence the labor force participation and employment status among various family members or household types? Answering these questions should greatly expand existing knowledge about the influence or role of such environments on Southeast Asian refugee households.

Questionnaire for Annual Survey of Refugees

OMB Number _____
Expiration Date _____

QUESTIONNAIRE FOR ANNUAL SURVEY OF REFUGEES

Office of Refugee Resettlement
Administration for Children and Families
Department of Health and Human Services

ASR-I
ENGLH

Household ID Number   _____
Interviewer's Name   _____ Code ___/___/___
Date of Interview   _____
Time Interview Started   _____ AM PM

ATTEMPTS TO CONTACT INTERVIEWEE

1. _____	5. _____	9. _____
2. _____	6. _____	10. _____
3. _____	7. _____	
4. _____	8. _____	

**TOTAL NUMBER OF ATTEMPTS TO CONTACT
INTERVIEWEE** _____

NAME OF RESPONDENT

LastMiddle	First

CURRENT ADDRESS

Street#	Street Name	Apt.#
CityState	Zip Code	

TELEPHONE

(_____) _____
Area Code

INTRODUCTORY STATEMENT

We are with Arrington Dixon and Associates. Inc. We are calling in connection with a survey that we are conducting for the U.S. Office of Refugee Resettlement concerning the adjustment to life in the United States refugees and certain other recent immigrants.

About two weeks ago we sent you a letter describing this survey. As indicated in that letter, any information that you give us will be held in confidence and will be used for statistical purposes only. Today we would like to talk to you further about your life in this country.

If you have no questions, we would like to proceed with the interview.

ORR-9

Public reporting burden for this collection of information is estimated to average 45 minutes per response.

Send comments regarding this burden estimate or any other aspect of this collection of information including suggestions for reducing this burden, to: Reports Clearance Office, Administration for Children and Families, Department of Health and Human Services, 370 L'Enfant Promenade, Washington, D.C. 20447; and to: Office of

Management and Budget, Paperwork Reduction Project, OMB Control No. _____, Washington. D.C. 20403.

Q.1　We would like to start by asking you a few questions about each person who live here, or who is staring or visiting here and has no other home. Let us start with the person who has overall responsibility, that is the person in whose name your home is rented, owned, or is being bought: the head of the household. (RECORD ANSWERS ON ATTACHED CONTROL CARD)

　　　a.　What is the name of the Head of the household, and of each of the other members of the household? (PROBE: ARE THERE OTHER PERSONS WHO USUALLY LIVE HERE BUT ARE TEMPORARILY ABSENT?)

FOR EACH HOUSEHOLD MEMBER ASK:

　　　b.　What is . . . relationship to the head of household?
　　　c.　What is . . . current marital status?
　　　　　01　Now married (note: spouse need not live in household)
　　　　　02　Divorced
　　　　　03　Legally separated
　　　　　04　Never married
　　　　　05　Widowed
　　　　　06　Other (SPECIFY)_____
　　　d.　What was . . . age at last birthday?
　　　e.　What was . . . date of birth?
　　　f.　is . . male or female?
　　　g.　What is . . . country of birth?
　　　h.　What is . . . country of citizenship?
　　　i.　What is . . ethnic origin?
　　　j.　What month and year did . . . enter the U.S. to stay?
　　　k.　In what State did . . . originally resettle?

New I want to ask some question only of person in your household who are 16 years old or older.

Q.2a　How many years of schooling did . . . complete before coming to the U.S.?

Q.2b   What was the highest degree or certificate that . . . obtained
        before coming to the U.S.?
        01 None
        02 Primary
        03 Training in refugee camp
        04 Technical school certification
        05 Secondary (or high school diploma)
        06 University degree (other than medical)
        07 Medical degree
        08 other (SPECIFY) _____
        (-9) DK/ (-8) RA/ (-7) NA

Q.3a   Before coming to the U.S., was . . .: (If in a refugee camp
        prior to type U.S., what type of employment did the person
        hold before that?)
        01 Not employed (skip to Q.3d)
        02 Civil servant (civilian in local or national government)
        03 in the military
        04 Employee in private sector
        05 Self-employed
        06 Student
        07 Other (SPECIFY)
        (-9) DK /(-8) RA/ (-7) NA

Q.3b   What kind of work (activities) did . . perform before coming
        to the U.S.? (e.g. . lawyer, typist, farmer, teacher, electrician,
        student)

Q.3c   What were the most important activities or duties in this job?

Q.3d   Was . . . in a prison or reeducation camp prior to coming to
        the U.S.?
        01 NO
        Yes. How long was . . . there?
        (-9) DK/(-8) RA/(-7) NA

Q.4a   At the time of snivel in the U.S., how well did . . . speak
        English?
        01 Very well
        02 Well

03 Not well
04 Not at all
(-9) DK/ (-8) RA/ (-7) NA

Q.4b How well does . . . speak English now?
01 Very well
02 Well
03 Not well
04 Not at all
(-9) DK/ (-8) RA/ (-7) NA

Q.4c Before coming to the U.S. did . . . have any English language instruction?
01 No (skip to Q.4e)
02 Yes
(-9) DK/ (-8) RA/ (-7) NA

Q.4d (If yes to e. 4c) Altogether how many weeks did . . . attend English language instruction before coming to the U.S.?

Q.4e Since coming to the U.S.. has . . . attended an English language training program?
01 No (slap to Q.5a)
02 Yes
03 High school student (skip to Q.5a)
(-9) DK/ (-8) RA/ (-7) NA

Q.4f How many weeks did . . attend English language training since coming to the U.S.?

Q.4g Did the English language class that . . . attended in the U.S. meet every day or less frequently?
01 Every day
02 2 to 6 times a week
03 Once a week
(-9) DK/ (-8) RA/ (-7) NA

Q.4h How many hours a day was . . . in that English language training?

Q.4I   Has . . . had any English language training in the U.S. in the
          past 12 months?
          01 No (skip to Q.5a)
          02 Yes
          (-9) DK/ (-8) RA/ (-7) NA

Q.4j   Is . . . currently enrolled in an English language training
          program?
          01 No
          02 Yes
          (-9) DK/ (-8) RA/ (-7) NA

Q.4k   What type of organization gave the English language training
          program? (Most recent program if more than one)
          01   School or university
          02   Employer program
          03   Religious organization
          04   Refugee service agency (state/local government)
          05   Refugee mutual assistance association (MAA)
          06   Private individual/Group
          07   Other (SPECIFY) _____
          (-9) DK/ (-8) RA/ (-7) NA

Q.5a   Did . . . work at a job anytime *last week*?
          01   No (skip to Q.11a)
          02   Yes (go to Q.5b)
          (-9) DK/ (-8) RA/ (-7) NA (skip to Q.11a)

(FOR PERSONS WHO WORKED LAST WEEK)

Q.5b   Did . . . work at more than one job *last week*?
          01   No (skip to Q.6a)
          02   Yes (go to Q.5c)
          (-9) DK/ (-8) RA/ (-7) NA (skip to Q.6a)

Q.5e   How many jobs did . . . work at *last week*?

Q.6a   How many hours did . . . work at his/her primary job *last
          week*? (Primary job means the job worked at for the greatest
          number of hours)

Q.6b   How many hours did . . . work at all jobs *last week*?

Q.7   How much money *per hour* did . . . receive at his/her primary job *last week*? (If knows hourly wage, skip Q.8a & Q8b. If not, continue with Q.8a.)

Q.8a How much did . . . earn before taxes from that job?

Q.8b On what basis is that amount computed?
    01   Weekly
    02   Bi-weekly
    03   Monthly
    04   Yearly
(If. . . worked at second job last week, ask Q.9)
(If . . . worked only one job last week, skip to Q. 18a)

(SECOND JOB ONLY)

Q.9   How much money per hour did . . . receive from his/her second job *last week*? (If knows hourly wage, skip to Q.18a. If not, continue with Q.10a)
Q.10a   How much did. . . earn before taxes from that job?
Q.10b   On what basis is that amount computed?
    01   Weekly
    02   Bi-weekly
    03   Monthly
    04   Yearly
    (skip to Q.18a)

(FOR PERSONS WHO DID NOT WORK LAST WEEK)

Q.11a   Has. . . ever worked since coming to the U.S. to stay?
    01   Never worked in the U.S. (skip to Q.13)
    02   Yes—How many weeks has it been since . . . had a job?
    (-9) DK/ (-8) RA/ (-7) NA

Q.11b   (If yes to 11a, other wise skip to Q.12) Since coming to the U.S., in how many weeks has . . ever worked?

Q.12   Was . . . temporarily absent or on layoff from a job or business last week?

01 No
02 Yes
(-9) DK/ (-8) RA/ (-7) NA

Q.13   Has been looking for work during the *last 4 weeks*?
01 No (skip to Q. 17)
02 Yes
(-9) DK/ (-8) RA/ (-7) NA (skip to Q. 17)

Q.14   What has . . . done to find a job? Has he/she checked with:
(multiple answer may be given)
01 Nothing
02 Refugee mutual assistance association (MAA)
03 Refugee service agency
04 Public employment agency
05 Private employment agency
06 Advertisements
07 Sponsor
08 Other refugees
09 Friends (not refugees)
11 Other (SPECIFY)
(-9) DK/ (-8) RA/ (-7) NA

Q.15   How many weeks has . . . been looking for a job?

Q.16   What caused . . . to begin looking for work? (*multiple answer may be given*)
01 New arrival in the U.S.
02 Lost job
03 Quit job
04 Finished school
05 Training ended
06 Moved to a new area
07 Medical problem ended
08 Other (SPECIFY)
09 Eligibility for cash and/or medical assistance ended
(-9) DK/ (-8) RA/ (-7) NA

(Skip to Q.18a IF WORKED; *OR* to Q.23a IF NEVER WORKED)

Q.17   Why is . . . not looking for a job? (*multiple answer may be given*)
    01   Limited English
    02   Attending school or training
    03   Poor health or handicap
    04   Child care or family responsibilities
    05   Believes no work is available
    06   Tried to find work but couldn't
    07   Other (SPECIFY) _____
    (-9) DK/ (-8) RA/ (-7) NA

(*FOR ALL PERSONS WHO HAD WORKED IN THE United States— IF DID NOT WORKLAST WEEK.ASK ABOUT LAST JOB) GO TO Q.23a IF INDIVIDUAL NEVER WORKED IN THE U.S.*

Q.18a   In the last year, how many weeks did . . . work?

Q.18b   How many hours per week did . . . usually work?

Q.18c   What were . . .'s total earnings before taxes from all jobs   in the past 12 months?

Q.18d   When did . . . get his/her first job in the U.S.?

Q.18e   Did the income that . . . received from his/her first job disqualify . . . from receiving cash assistance (*such as RCA, AFDC, or GA*)?
    01   No
    02   Yes
    03   Was not receiving cash assistance at that time
    (-9) DK/ (-8) RA/ (-7) NA

Q.19b   What kind of business or industry is this? (e.g., hospital, electronic parts manufacturing, social service agency)
Q.19e   What Kind of work does(did) . . perform? (e.g., nurse, assembly line worker, typist, supervisor)
Q.20   Is (was) . . . a:
    01   Employee of a private company, business, or individual (*go to Q.22a*)
    02   Federal government employee (*go to Q.22a*)

03　State government employee (*go to Q.22a*)
04　Local government employee (*go to Q.22a*)
05　Self-employed (*go to Q.21*)
06　Working without pay in family business (*skip to Q.23a*)
07　Other (SPECIFY)＿＿＿＿＿＿＿
(-9) DK/ (-8) RA/ (-7) NA

Q.21　[IFSELF-EMPLOYED]
a.　What kind of business is it? (e.g., restaurant, tailor shop, grocery store)
b.　How many other refugees does . . . employ?
c.　How many total employees does . . . have?

[FOR EMPLOYEE ONLY]

Q.22a　What did. . . do to find this job? Did he/she check with:
01　Voluntary agency(agency that helped with initial U.S. resettlement)
02　Refugee mutual assistance association (MAA)
03　Refugee service agency
04　Public Employment Agency
05　Private Employment Agency
06　Advertisements
07　Sponsor
08　Other refugees
09　Friends (not refugees)
11　Other (SPECIFY)＿＿＿＿＿
(-9) DK/ (-8) RA/ (-7) NA

Q.22b　How many other refugees are employed there?

Q.23a　How many cars, vans or small trucks are kept at home that . . . could use to get to work, job-training or school? (or that another household member could use to drive . . . to such activities)
01　None
02　One
03　Two or more
(-9) DK/ (-8) RA/ (-7) NA

Q.23b   Is there a bus stop, subway station, or other public transportation stop within a mile of this housing unit that . . . could use to get to work or other activities?
01 No
02 Yes
(-9) DK/ (-8) RA/ (-7) NA

Q.24a   Has. . .attended any job-training program since coming to the United States?
01 No (skip to Q.25a)
02 Yes
(-9) DK/ (-8) RA/ (-7) NA

Q.24b   How many weeks did that training last?

Q.24c   Did the job-training class meet every day or less frequently?
01 Every day
02 2 to 6 times a week
03 Once a week

Q.24d   How many hours a day did the job-training class meet?

Q.24e   For what kind of work (occupation) did this training prepare . . .? (*e.g., electronics assembler, welder, typist, nurse, childcare provider*)

Q.25a   Has . . . attended school or university (other than to take English language training or the job-training class indicated in the previous question) since coming to the U.S.?
01 No (skip to Q.26a)
02 Yes
(-9) DK/ (-8) RA/ (-7) NA

Q.25b   Was . . . attending school or university in order to obtain a degree or certificate?
01 No (skip to Q.26a)
02 Yes
(-9) DK/ (-8) RA/ (-7) NA

Q.25c   What degree or certificate was . . . attempting to earn?

01 High school certificate or equivalency
02 Associate degree
03 Bachelor's degree
04 Master's or Doctorate degree
05 Professional school degree (*e.g., MD, LLB, DDS*)
06 Other (SPECIFY) _____
(-9) DK/ (-8) RA/ (-7) NA

Q.25d   Has . . . received this degree or certificate?
        01 No (skip to Q.26a)
        02 Yes
        (-9) DK/ (-8) RA/ (-7) NA

Q.25e   In what year did . . . receive this degree or certificate?

Q.26a   How many months elapsed between the time . . . left his/her
        native country and the time . . . arrived in the U.S.?

Q.26b   How many months has . . . lived at this residence?

Q.26c   Did . . . live at this residence a year ago?
        01 No
        02 Yes(*skip to Q.27a*)
        (-9) DK/ (-8) RA/ (-7) NA

Q.26d   Did . . . live in this state a year ago?
        01 No
        02 Yes(*skip to Q.27a*)
        (-9) DK/ (-8) RA/ (-7) NA

Q.26e   In which state did . . . live a year ago?
        01 Not in the U. S.(*skip to Q.27a*)
        Specify state
        (-9) DK/ (-8) RA/ (-7) NA

Q.26f   What was the primary reason that . . . moved to this state?

Q.27a   (*For persons in the U.S. 12 months or longer*): Has . . .
        applied to adjust his/her immigration status to that of a
        permanent U.S. resident?

01   No (skip to Q.27c)
02   Yes (ask Q.27b)
(-9) DK/ (-8) RA/ (-7) NA

Q.27b   When did . . . apply for adjustment to permanent resident status7 *(If application date is given, skip to Q.28)*

Q.27c   Does . . . plan to adjust his/her immigration status in the future?
01   No
02   Yes
03   Did not know he/she had to apply to become a permanent resident
(-9) DK/ (-8) RA/ (-7) NA

Q.28   Does this person have a physical, mental, or other health condition that has lasted for 6 or more months and which:
a.   Limits the kind or amount of work this person can do at a job?
01   No
02   Yes
(-9) DK/ (-8) RA/ (-7) NA
b.   Prevents this person from working at a job?
01   No
02   Yes
(-9) DK/ (-8) RA/ (-7) NA

Q.29a   During the past 12 months, how were . . .'s medical expenses paid? *(may indicate more than one)*
01   No medical expenses
02   Self or household members
03   Other relatives or friends
04   Sponsor/sponsoring agency
05   Religious organization
06   Medicaid or Refugee medical assistance
07   Other government source
08   Insurance through own employment *(e.g., Blue Cross)*
09   Insurance through family member's employment
11   Other source (SPECIFY) _____
(-9) DK/ (-8) RA/ (-7) NA

Q.29b What is . . . usual source of medical care?
    01 No regular source
    02 Private physician
    03 Emergency room at a hospital
    04 Health clinic
    05 Folk healer
    06 Other (SPECIFY) _____
    (-9) DK/ (-8) RA/ (-7) NA

Q.29c Was there any time in the past 12 months when . . . was not covered either by refugee medical assistance, Medicaid, or private health insurance?
    01 Covered in all months
    02 Yes—number of months not covered: _____
        (-1) Not covered 1 month or less
        (-3) Not covered in any month (*Skip to Q.30a*)

Q.29d What type of health insurance coverage did . . . have in the past 12 months? (*indicate all that apply*)
    01 Insurance through own or family member's employment
    02 Private insurance unrelated to employment
    03 Medicaid or refugee medical assistance
    04 Other government health care
    05 Other insurance (SPECIFY) _____
    (-9) DK/ (-8) RA/ (-7) NA

Now we would like to ask a few questions about the household.

Q.30a **FOOD STAMPS**—In the past 12 months, have one or more persons in your household received food stamps?
    01 No(skip to Q.31a)
    02 Yes
    (-9) DK/ (-8) RA/ (-7) NA (skip to Q.31a)

Q.30b Who received them? (circle person #s in whose name the assistance was received)

Q.30c What was the total cash value per month? (*household*)

Q.30d How many months in the past 12 months were food stamps received?

Q.31a **AFDC**—In the past 12 months, have one or more persons in your household received cash assistance through the Aid to Families with Dependent Children (AFDC) program?
01 No (skip to Q.31f)
02 Yes
(-9) DK/ (-8) RA/ (-7) NA (skip to Q.31f)

Q.31b Which household members received such assistance? (circle person #s in whose name the assistance was received)

Q.31c What was the cash amount received each month? (*household*)

Q.31d How many months in the past 12 months was the AFDC received?

Q.31e In which specific months was AFDC received?
9   10   11   12   1   2   3   4   5   6   7   8
(e.g., 9 = previous September)

Q.31f Since coming to the United States, in how many months one or more persons in your household received AFDC?
(A) Every month
(B) No months
(C) Number of months: _____
(-9) DK/ (-8) RA/ (-7) NA

Q.32a **CA**—In the past 12 months, have one or more persons in your household received assistance through the Refugee Cash Assistance (RCA) program?
01 No (skip to Q.33a)
02 Yes
(-9) DK/ (-8) RA/ (-7) NA (skip to Q.33a)

Q.32b Which household members received such assistance? (*circle person #s in whose name the assistance was received*)

Q.32c What was the cash amount received each month? (*household*)

Q.32d   How many months in the past 12months was RCA received?

Q.32e   In which specific months was RCA received?
        9   10   11   12   1   2   3   4   5   6   7   8
        (e.g., 9 = previous September)

Q.33a   **SSI**—In the past 12 months, have one or more persons in
        your household received Supplemental Security Income
        (SSI)?
        01   No (skip to Q.33f)
        02   Yes
        (-9) DK/ (-8) RA/ (-7) NA (skip to Q.33f)

Q.33b   Which household members received such assistance? (circle
        person #s in whose name the assistance was received)

Q.33c   What was the cash amount received each month? (household)

Q.33d   How many months in the past 12 months was SSI received?

Q.33e   In which specific months was SSI received?
        9   10   11   12   1   2   3   4   5   6   7   8
        (e.g., 9 = previous September)

Q.33f   Since coming to the U.S., in how many months have one or
        more persons in your household received SSI?
        (A) Every month
        (B) No months
        Number of months: _____
        (-9) DK/ (-8) RA/ (-7) NA

Q.34a   **GA**—In the past 12 months, have one or more persons in
        your household received income from General Assistance
        (GA)?
        01   No (skip to Q.34f)
        02   Yes
        (-9) DK/ (-8) RA/ (-7) NA (skip to Q.34f)

Q.34b   Which household members received such assistance7 (circle
        person #s in whose name the assistance was received)

Q.34c   What was the cash amount received each month? (household)

Q.34d   How many months in the past 12months was GA received?

Q.34e   In which specific months was GA received?
9   10   11   12   1   2   3   4   5   6   7   8
(e.g., 9 = previous September)

Q.34f   Since coming to the U.S., in how many months have one or more persons in your household received GA?
(A) Every month
(B) No months
Number of months: _____
(-9) DK/ (-8) RA/ (-7) NA

Q.35a   **CASH**—In the past 12 months, have one or more persons in your household received cash assistance directly from a voluntary agency, sponsor, religiousorganization, or MAA?
01   No(skip to Q.36a)
02   Yes
(-9) DK/ (-8) RA/ (-7) NA (skip to Q.36a)

Q.35b   What type of organization or person gave such assistance?
01   Voluntary agency
02   Religious organization
03   Refugee mutual assistance association (MAA)
04   Sponsor
05   Other individual or family member
(-9) DK/ (-8) RA/ (-7) NA

Q.35c   Which household members received such assistance? (circle person #s in whose name the assistance was received)

Q.35d   What was the cash amount received each month? (*household*)

Q.35e   How many months in the past 12 months was this private assistance received?

Q.36a   **OTHER INCOME**—Within the past 12 months has anyone in the household received income from any other source on a regular basis (such as interest from savings accounts, net rental income, child support, unemployment compensation or retirement income)l

01   No (skip to Q.37)
02   Yes
(-9) DK/ (-8) RA/ (-7) NA

Q.36b   Who received the income? (circle person #s in whose name income was received)

Q.36c   What was the cash amount received on average each month? (household)

Q.36d   How many months was this income received in the past 12 months?

Q.36f   What was the source of that income? (more than one answer can be given)
01   Interest income
02   Net rental income
03   Child support
04   Unemployment compensation
05   Retirement income
06   Other (SPECIFY) _____
(-9) DK/ (-8) RA/ (-7) NA

Q.38a   Is this house or apartment
01   Rented for cash rent
02   Owned by you or someone in this household with or without a mortgage or loan
03   Occupied without payment of cash rent
(-9) DK/ (-8) RA/ (-7) NA

Q.38b   How much is the total monthly payment for this housing unit7 (For owners, include total mortgage payment, taxes, insurance and utilities; for renters include rent plus utilities— gas, electricity and heating oil—if paid separately)

Q.38c   Is this housing unit in a public housing project that is, is it owned by a local housing authority or other local public agency?
01   No
02   Yes

(-9) DK/ (-8) RA/ (-7) NA

THAT WAS OUR FINAL QUESTION. THANK YOU VERY MUCH FOR YOUR PARTICIPATION IN THIS SURVEY.

INTERVIEWER: Remember to answer the questions on the following page.

FOR INTERVIEWER ONLY
A. Time Interview Ended _____ AM PM
B. General Responsiveness of Respondent
   01 Willing
   02 Neutral
   03 Reluctant
C. List Difficulties, if any, With the Interview

_____
_____
_____
_____
_____

D. Language in which Interview was Conducted
E. Interviewer's Ethnicity

(D)	(E)
01 Russian	01 Russian
02 Vietnamese	02 Vietnamese
03 Laotian	03 Lao
04 Cambodian	04 Cambodian
05 H'mong	05 H'mong
06 Spanish	06 Cuban/other Hispanic
07 Amharic	07 Ethiopian
08 Creole	08 Chinese
09 Chinese	09 Chinese
10 Romanian	10 Romanian
11 Polish	11 Polish
12 Armenian	12 Armenian
13 Ukrainian	13 Ukrainian
14 Arabic	14 Iraqi
15 Farsi	15 Iranian
16 Afghan	16 Afghan

17 English 17 Khmer
18 Other (SPECIFY) _____ 18 Other (SPECIFY) _____
END

Bibliography

Angel, R. & Tienda, M. (1982). Determinants of Extended Household Structure: Cultural Patterns or Economic Need? *American Journal of Sociology, 87*(6), 360-83.

Babbie, E. (1990). *Survey Research Methods.* Belmont, CA: Wadworth Publishing.

Bach, R. L. & Argiros, R. (1991). Economic Progress Among Southeast Asian Refugees in the United States. In H. Adelman (Ed.), *Refugee Policy, Canada and the United States* (pp.322-343). Staten Island, NY: Center for Migration Studies.

Bach, R. L. & Carroll-Seguin R. (1986). Labor Force Participation, Household Composition and Sponsorship among Southeast Asian Refugee. *International Migration Review, 20*(2), 381-404.

Becker, S. G. (1993). *Human Capital: A Theoretical and Empirical Analysis, with Special Reference to Education.* Chicago, IL: The University of Chicago Press.

Blau, D. M. and Robins, P. K. (1989). Fertility, Employment, and Child-care Costs. *Demography, 26* (2), 287-299.

Caplan, N., Whitmore, J. K., and Bui, Q. L. (1985). *Southeast Asian Refugee Self-sufficiency Study: Final Report.* The Institute for Social Research, The University of Michigan.

Caplan, N., Whitmore, J. K., and Choy, M. H. (1990). *The Boat People and Achievement in America, A study of Economic and Education Success.* Ann Arbor, MI: The University of Michigan Press.

Carmines, E. G. & Zeller, R. A. (1977). *Reliability and Validity Assessment.* Series of Quantitative Applications in the Social Sciences. Beverly Hills, CA: SAGE.

Chiswick, B R.. (1979). The Economic Progress of Immigrants: Some Apparently Universal Patterns. In W. Fellner (Ed.), *Contemporary Economic Problems 1979* (pp. 357-99). Washington, D.C.: American Enterprise Institute.

Dickens, W. T. and Lang, K. (1985). A Test of Dual Labor Market Theory. *American Economic Review*, *75*(4), 792-805.

Dickens, W. T. and Lang, K. (1993). Labor Market Segmentation Theory: Reconsidering The Evidence. In W. Darity (Ed.), *Labor Economics: Problems in Analyzing Labor Markets* (pp.141-80). Norwell, MA: Kluwer Academic Publishers.

Floge, L. (1989). Changing Household Structure, Child-Care Availability, and Employment among Mothers of Preschool Children. *Journal of Marriage and the Family*, *51*(1), 51-63.

Ferber, M. A. & O'Farrell, B. (Eds.). (1991). *Work and Family: Policies for a Changing Work Force*. Panel on Employer Policies and Working Families, Committee on Women's Employment and Related social Issues, Commission on Behavioral and Social Sciences and Education National Research Council. Washington, D.C.: National Academy Press.

Gold, S. J. (1988). Refugees and Small Business: The Case of Soviet Jews and Vietnamese. *Ethnic and Racial Studies*, *11*(4), 411-38.

Gordon, L. W. (1989). National Surveys of Southeast Asian Refugee: Methods, Findings, Issues. In D. W. Haines (Ed.), *Refugee as Immigrants: Cambodians, Laotians and Vietamese in America* (pp. 24-39). Totowa, NJ: Rowman & Littlefield Publishers, Inc.

Greenwald, D. (1994). *The McGraw-Hill Encyclopedia of Economics*. New York, NY: McGraw-Hill.

Haines, D. W. (1988). Kinship in Vietnamese Refugee Resettlement: A Review of the U.S. Experience. *Journal of Comparative Family Studies*, *19*(1), 1-16.

Haines, D. W. (1989). Introduction. In D. W. Haines (Ed.), Refugee as Immigrants: *Cambodians, Laotians and Vietamese in America* (pp. 1-23). Totowa, NJ: Rowman & Littlefield Publishers, Inc.

Hardy, M. A. (1993). *Regression with Dummy Variables*. Newbury Park, CA: Sage Publications.

Hing, B. O. (1993). *Making and Remaking Asian America Through Immigration Policy 1850-1990*. Stanford, CA: Stanford University Press.

Jensen, L. (1991). Secondary Earner Strategies and Family Poverty: Immigrant-native Differentials, 1960-1980. *International Migration Review*, *25*(1), 113-39.

Kerpen, K. S. (1985). Refugees on Welfare, Is The Dependency Rate Really a Problem?. *Public Welfare*, Winter, 21-25.

Kibria, N. (1994). Household Structure and Family Ideologies: The Dynamics of Immigrant Economic Adaptation Among Vietnamese Refugees. *Social Problems*, 41(1), 81-96.

Kim, Y. Y. (1989). Personal, Social, and Economic Adaptation: 1975-1979 Arrivals in Illinois. In D. W. Haines (Ed.), *Refugee as Immigrants: Cambodians, Laotians and Vietamese in America* (pp.86-104). Totowa, NJ: Rowman & Littlefield Publishers, Inc.

Le-Doux, C. & Stephens, K. S. (1992). Refugee and Immigrant Social Service Delivery: Critical Management Issues. *Journal of Multicultural Social Work*, 2(1). 31-45.

Lee, S. M. & Edmonston B. (1994). The Socioeconomic Status and Integration of Asian Immigrants. In B. Edmonston & J. S. Passel (Eds.), *Immigration and Ethnicity, The Integration of America's Newest Arrivals* (pp. 101-138). Washington, D.C.: The Urban Institute Press.

Light, I., Sabagh, G., Bozorgmehr M., and Der-Martirosian. C. (1994). Beyond the Ethnic Enclave Economy. *Social Problems*, 41(1), 65-80.

Majka, L. & Mullan, B. (1992). Employment Retention, Area of Origin and Type of Social Support among Refugees in the Chicago Area. *International Migration Review*, 26(3), 899-926.

Marshall, F. R. & Briggs, V. M. Jr. (1989). *Labor Economics: Theory, Institutions, and Public Policy*. Boston, MA: IRWIN, Inc.

Menard, S. (1995). *Applied Logistic Regression Analysis*. Thousand Oaks, CA: Sage Publication.

Mincer, J. (1960). Labor Supply, Family Income and Consumption. *American Economic Review*, 50(May), 574-83.

Moen, P. & Wethington, E. (1992). The Concept of Family Adaptive Strategies. *Annual Review of Sociology*, 18, 233-51.

OSI (Opportunity Systems, Incorporated). (1981). *Ninth Wave Report: Indochinese Resettlement Operational Feedback*. Washington, D.C.

Pedraza, S. (1994). Introduction from the Special Issue Editor: The Sociology of Immigration, Race, and Ethnicity in America. *Social Problems*, 41(1), 1-8.

Perez, L. (1986). Immigrant Economic Adjustment and family Organization: The Cuban Success Story Reexamined. *International Migration Review*, 20(1), 4-20.

Pfeffer, M. J. (1994). Low-Wage Employment and Ghetto Poverty: A Comparison of African-American and Cambodian Day-Haul Farm Workers in Philadelphia. *Social Problems*, 41(1), 9-29.

Portes, A. & Stepick, A. (1985). Unwelcome Immigrants: The Labor Market Experiences of 1980(Mariel) Cuban and Haitian Refugees in South Florida. *American Sociological Review* , *50*, 493-514.

Potocky, M. (1996). Refugee Resettlement in the United States: Implications for International social Welfare. *Journal of Sociology and Social Welfare*, 163-174.

Potocky, M. & McDonald, T. P. (1995). Predictors of economic status of Southeast Asian refugees: Implications for service improvement. *Social Work Research, 19*(4), 219-227.

Rodriguez, H. (1992). Household Composition, Employment Patterns, and Income Inequality: Puerto Ricans in the New York and Other Areas of the U.S. Mainland. *Hispanic Journal of Behavioral Sciences, 14* (1), 52-75.

Rosen, S. (1987). Human Capital. In J. Eatwell, M. Milgate, and P. Newman (Eds.), *The New Palgrave: A Dictionary of Economics* (pp. 681-690). New York, NY: The Stockton Press.

Rumbaut, R. G. (1989). Portraits, Patterns, and Predictors of the Refugee Adaptation Process: Results and Reflections from the IHARP Panel Study. In D. W. Haines (Ed.), *Refugee as Immigrants: Cambodians, Laotians and Vietamese in America* (pp. 138-182). Totowa, NJ: Rowman & Littlefield Publishers, Inc.

Sanders, W. B. & Pinhey, T. K. (1983). *The conduct of Social Reserarch.* New York, NY: CBS College Publishing

Skolnick, A. (1995). Nuclear Family. In D. Levinson (Ed.) *Encyclopedia of marriage and the family* (pp. 518-520). New York, NY: Simon & Schuster Macmillan. .

SPSS. 1992. *SPSS/PC+ Advanced Statistics^{TM}, Version 5.0.* Chicago, IL: SPSS Inc.

Stolzenberg, R. M. (1975). Occupations, Labor Markets and the Process of Wage Attainment. *American Sociological Review, 40*, 645-665.

Tienda, M. and Glass, J. (1985). Household Structure and Labor force Participation of Black, Hispanic, and White Mothers. *Demography* , *22*(3), 381-94.

Tiggs, L. M. (1988). Age, Earnings, and Change Within the Dual Economy. *Social Forces, 66*(3), 676-698.

U.S. Committee for Refugees. (1992). Refugee Reports interview with ORR director Chris Gersten. *Refugee Reports, 13*(10), 6-10.

U.S. Department of Commerce (US DC). Economics and Statistics Administration, Bureau of the Census. 1991 and 1992. *Statistical Abstract of the United States, The National Data Book.* Washington, D.C.: The U.S. Government Printing Office.

U.S. Department of Health and Human Services, Office of Refugee Resettlement (ORR). (1990), (1994), and (1995). *Annual Report to Congress, Refugee Resettlement Program.* Washington, DC: The U.S. Government Printing Office.

U.S. Department of Health and Human Services, Social Security Administration (SSA), Office of Research and Statistics. (1993). Social Security Programs in the United States. *Social Security Bulletin, 56*(4), 80.

Wagner, R. A. (1995). Extended Family. In D. Levinson (Ed.), *Encyclopedia of marriage and the family* (pp. 238-241). New York, NY: Simon & Schuster Macmillan.

Waldinger, R. (1984). The Occupational and Economic Integration of the New Immigrants. In R. R. Hofstetter (Ed.), *U.S. Immigration Policy* (pp. 197-222). Durham, NC: Duke University Press.

Wilson, K. L. & Portes, A. (1980). Immigrant Enclaves: An Analysis of the Labor Market Experience of Cubans in Miami. *American Journal of Sociology, 86*, 295-319.

Wong, R. & Levine, R. E. (1992). The Effect of Household Structure on Women's Economic Activity and Fertility: Evidence from Recent Mothers in Urban Mexico. *Economic Development and Cultural Change, 41*(1), 89-102.

Wooden, M. (1991). The Experience of Refugees in the Australian Labor Market. *International Migration Review , 25*(3), 514-35.

Index

NAME